surreal
gourmet bites

surreal gourmet bites

showstoppers and conversation starters

by **bob blumer** (a.k.a. the surreal gourmet)

photographs by **suzi q. varin**

CHRONICLE BOOKS

SAN FRANCISCO

Library of Congress Cataloging-in-Publication Data available.

ISBN 0-8118-4512-5

Manufactured in China.

Designed by Sara Cambridge
Prop styling by Bob Blumer and Suzi Q. Varin
Food styling by Bob Blumer
Typesetting by Sara Cambridge
Toastermobile Portrait by George Whiteside

10 9 8 7 6 5 4 3 2 1

Chronicle Books LLC
85 Second Street
San Francisco, California 94105

www.chroniclebooks.com

Page 2: bang-bang drummettes, page 72

|||||||||||||||||||||

For my fellow gastronauts.

|||||||||||||||||||||

table of contents

veggies

sweets

fodder

introduction

Without really being conscious that an evolution had taken place, I realized recently that the appetizers, entrées, and desserts I used to serve at my dinner parties had morphed into what I have come to call "flights of bites." A flight of bites, as I define it, is a parade of one- and two-bite offerings. The format borrows liberally from the Spanish world of tapas and the now common practice of restaurant grazing (sampling a variety of appetizers, usually at the bar, at a succession of restaurants). Being the Surreal Gourmet, I've taken the concept one step further by creating tiny dishes that pleasure the palate *and* amuse the eye.

Looking back, the bite that started it all was a coconut shrimp lollypop (page 37) I created for my Food Network show. It's a pinwheeled shrimp, dipped in batter, dredged in freshly grated coconut shreds, and deep fried into a golden brown ball. As the name suggests, it is presented on a stick. I served these skewered into a watermelon wedge, alongside an Asian-inspired apricot dipping sauce. The kudos these lollypops garnered took me by surprise. The intense flavors and whimsical presentation twist elevated the common ingredients from ho-hum appetizer status to a wow-inspiring special treat. Since then I have been obsessed with developing new recipes and mining my repertoire in search of dishes that can be reconfigured and condensed into tiny creative packages.

These bites are unbelievably flexible. One is guaranteed to deify anybody who brings it to a party. Two can jump-start a fabulous meal and create a halo effect around the host. And five or six will work beautifully for a dinner party or a cocktail party as a complete menu. In any configuration, they are guaranteed to be showstoppers and conversation starters.

form

I find visual inspiration everywhere: In functional industrial design; on billboards; in my travels; in the art of Dalí, Magritte, Warhol, and even Dr. Seuss. If there is one common denominator, it is that all of these sources of inspiration have minimal barriers to entry. I try to keep my food presentation accessible as well. Virtually all of the dishes in this book are presented on unadorned (albeit beautiful) plates, in common disposable containers, on bamboo skewers, in basic shot glasses, and/or in edible containers. Some of them are my own invention and some are classic dishes that I have put my own spin on. In the world of food fetishes, shooting back gazpacho from a sculpted cucumber cup is far more exhilarating than eating it from a bowl with a soup spoon.

Once you have mastered each recipe, you can (should you choose) present it in exactly the same manner as I have. But don't stop there. There are plenty of common household objects surrounding you that are just waiting to be repurposed. Use small mirrors, glass shelving, a (new) galvanized garbage can lid, children's toys, take-out containers, caviar tins, Krispy Kreme boxes, or whatever else you can find, and put your own whimsical spin on the presentation.

function

Most of the dishes in this book have been designed to work in a cocktail party environment, a few are better suited to being eaten sitting down with proper cutlery, and many swing both ways. This serving concept is infinitely easier for anybody with an open kitchen (and I highly recommend the use of a sledgehammer for anyone with a walled-in kitchen who loves to cook and entertain at the same time). However, with a little planning and foresight, anyone in any kitchen can create a dinner of small bites.

I can't change the oil in my car to save my life, and I can't differentiate between RAM and hard drive space on my laptop, so I can totally empathize with anyone who is intimidated in the kitchen. Regardless of your kitchen comfort level, here are a few tips for planning a dinner party of small bites.

The first step is to construct a menu that suits your culinary abilities, comfort level, facilities, and resources. As with comedy, timing is everything. Select dishes that can be completed well in advance and pair them with those that require last-minute attention. (This is crucial, especially for cooks without the aforementioned open kitchen—and for those of you who do not believe the world is a stage.) Pick your showstoppers, and then balance the menu with supporting acts as well as extras like store-bought dips or desserts.

Whether you are having a casual get-together, a cocktail party, or a sit-down dinner, my experience is that most guests will make the event the one-stop destination for all their dining needs (blackout dates for this rule-of-thumb include December 1–24 and New Year's Eve). When planning how much food to serve, some general rules apply:

- About four savory and two sweet dishes make a meal.
- Plan on two portions of each savory bite per person (those who don't like, or eat, any one particular bite will be balanced out by the big eaters who come back for more). One of each dessert bite should suffice.
- Increase portions by 50% when hosting sumo wrestlers, lumberjacks, or college students.

As important and rewarding as it is to create an impressive menu, your spirit can have an equal influence on the overall success of the evening. My mantra is simple: Guests feed off your energy as much as your food. Repeat this to yourself as you embark on your adventures in entertaining.

environment

In every episode of my television show, I arrive in my Toastermobile at a new location and reconfigure the available space into a vibrant dinner party environment. I've thrown dinner parties at a construction site, a fire station, a hockey arena, and even in a laundromat. Each party has had its own distinctive energy and excitement. Sure it's TV—but it's cable—which means that the available planning time, manpower, and budgets are only a smidgen more than they would be in real life. All the dinner parties I've hosted during the three seasons of my show, as well as the hundreds I have cooked for in places other than my own home, have led me to conclude that there is no such thing as an inadequate space for a dinner party. In fact, I've found that overcoming the limitations of the surroundings contributes to the spirit and spontaneity of the evening.

liquids

Life for the hedonist is a game of vice management. One by one, I have discontinued my various guilty pleasures and refocused all of my obsessive-compulsive behavior on one source of pleasure: Wine (OK, there may be one more, but that's for another book). One of the manifestations of this behavior is my endless quest for symbiotic food and wine pairings. Call me a control freak (and many have) but when I throw a dinner party, I like to confiscate the wines that my guests bring, and match them with the bites from my menu. Then I fill in the blanks from my own cellar. One bottle of wine can easily be stretched across as many as twelve people, allowing everyone to have a taste of a harmonious wine and food pairing.

When I throw a cocktail party, I like to accompany each tray of bites with a tray of two-ounce pony glasses, which I fill with a small taste of a wine, port, sake, liquor, or liqueur that complements the flavors in the food.

As your self-appointed sommelier, I've recommended (where appropriate) a wine varietal or other drink for each bite.

flavor

I am obsessed with flavor—the kind of big, bold flavor that knocks you off your feet, then bodyslams you to the mat as you struggle to regain your senses. That kind of flavor comes from great ingredients. And great ingredients come from smart shopping. No matter where you shop, if you buy ingredients at the bottom of the processed-food chain, and at the peak of their flavor and freshness, they will heighten the flavor quotient of everything you make and do a lot of the hard work for you.

In conventional grocery stores, inspired shopping is one part resourcefulness and one part sheer determination. Leave your inhibitions behind and scrutinize for freshness by prodding and smelling. And make the butcher and produce person your allies—they can do lots for you. Just by asking, they'll repackage portions, give you special cuts, and point you to the best values.

At farmers' markets, many of the vendors are the actual farmers themselves. When they detect even a flicker of interest in their produce, they usually become a fountain of information on everything from selection and storage to recipes.

Some of the ingredients called for in this book are quite specific, and not available in every grocery store. Let your fingers do the walking, plan ahead, patronize ethnic and specialty food shops—and if necessary, get creative. If you live in a small town where Asian ingredients such as wonton wrappers are unavailable, pick some up on your next visit to the big city and freeze them, or march into your local Chinese restaurant and ask to buy a few. When all else fails, order it over the Web. With Google and FedEx, the world is your oyster Rockefeller.

fish

haiku halibut

Sometimes inspiration comes on the installment plan. This spa-worthy dish was inspired by Nobu Matsuhisa's famous miso black cod, and an inventive cucumber salad I had at the Post Ranch Inn in Big Sur. The payoff is an elegant bite (or three) of clean, fresh flavors and textures.

halibut

10-ounce fillet of halibut, black cod, salmon, or Chilean sea bass (if it ever comes off the endangered list)

¼ cup miso paste

¼ cup sake

½ cup mirin (a sweet Japanese cooking wine)

1 tablespoon peanut or canola oil

1 tablespoon toasted sesame seeds

cucumber noodles

1 tablespoon toasted sesame oil

1 tablespoon freshly squeezed lime juice

1 teaspoon soy sauce

2 cucumbers (ideally the English variety), **peeled**

2 green onions, thinly sliced

3 tablespoons finely diced fresh mint leaves

Cut twelve ¾-inch cubes from the fish fillet.

In a medium bowl, add miso and 2 tablespoons sake. Blend with a whisk, then slowly blend in remaining sake and mirin. Transfer marinade to a resealable plastic bag, add fish, squeeze out air, and seal. Refrigerate for 4 hours.

In a medium bowl, whisk together oil, lime juice, and soy. Reserve. (This is the dressing for cucumber noodles.)

Just before cooking fish, make cucumber noodles. If using English cucumbers, cut them in half widthwise. Field cucumbers should be left whole.

Using a mandoline with a comblike julienne blade, shred the cucumber into spaghetti-like strips. Do this by running the sides of the cucumber, in one long movement from top to bottom, over the blade repeatedly until you get to the seeded part. Rotate the cucumber and continue shredding until all that is left is the squared-off seeded core. Discard the core. If you do not have a mandoline, improvise by using a sharp knife to cut the cucumber into matchstick-sized slices. In a medium bowl, toss cucumber with dressing, green onions, and mint.

Remove fish from marinade and reserve marinade. In a sauté pan over medium-high heat, add oil and pan sear fish for 2 minutes. Turn once and cook for 30 seconds on opposite side, or until cooked throughout, yet still moist. Remove and reserve fish.

Add $1/2$ cup of marinade to the pan. Reduce for 3 minutes, or until the thickness of maple syrup.

To assemble, twist a small mound of cucumber noodles around a fork (as though it were spaghetti) and set it in the center of a small plate. Top with a fish cube, drizzle a few drops of reduced marinade overtop, and sprinkle with a few sesame seeds.

uncommon goods a mandoline with a julienne attachment (available at most kitchen stores, starting at $20); miso (available in Asian markets, natural foods stores, and some grocery stores); mirin; sake

level of difficulty Your only hurdle is making the cucumber noodles. Once you have the mandoline, you are home free.

active prep 40 minutes

inactive prep 4 hours

cooking time 6 minutes

shortcuts Skip the cucumber noodles and serve the miso-marinated fish on a slice of cucumber that is drizzled with the sesame, lime, and soy dressing.

advance work The fish will actually benefit from being marinated up to 24 hours in advance. The cucumber noodles lose their water content quickly and must be made no more than 30 minutes in advance of being served. This is a great task to schluff off on any guest who naively volunteers to help.

music to cook by Puffy AmiYumi, *Nice* is a sugary sweet Japanese pop sensation.

liquid assets Roughly filtered (cloudy) sake, served cold, is the next big thing in Asian fusion cuisine. It has pure flavors of melon and coconut, which work in harmony with the fish and the cucumber.

psychedelic caviar

Fluorescent green and orange are the new black. At least they made a bold statement at the birthday extravaganza of a friend of mine who wanted to serve caviar to fifty guests without breaking the bank. The solution I created plays off the tradition of sevruga but uses the funky and affordable Japanese green wasabi caviar in its place. The result is so stimulating to the eye and explosive on the palate that it will turn heads at any event.

3 lemons, thinly sliced, seeds discarded

2 tablespoons peeled and grated fresh ginger, reserved in a small bowl to save any juice

2 ounces green wasabi caviar

1 ounce salmon roe

Line a large plate or a small baking sheet with wax paper. Select your 12 most aesthetically pleasing lemon slices and spread them out in a single layer. Freeze for 1 hour, or until frozen solid.

Set a small strainer over a small bowl. Transfer ginger to the strainer. Using the back of a spoon, extract the ginger juice by pressing the grated ginger against the strainer. Discard the solids and reserve the juice.

To assemble, remove lemon slices from the freezer just before serving and brush or drizzle a small amount of ginger juice on the top sides. Spoon 1/2 teaspoon of wasabi caviar into the center of each lemon slice. Top with a few salmon eggs. Instruct your guests to suck the caviar off the lemon slices (or better still, demonstrate for them).

uncommon goods wasabi caviar (available at caviar stores, specialty stores, and some Japanese groceries); salmon roe (available in most grocery stores)

the adventure club Start with one layer of sevruga caviar, then add wasabi and salmon roe.

level of difficulty On a scale of 1 to 10 these are a 1.

active prep 15 minutes

inactive prep 1 hour

shortcuts Skip the ginger drizzle.

advance work Lemon slices can be frozen eons in advance. Since caviar is traditionally the first thing served at a party, the bites can be assembled just before your guests arrive and refrigerated on the serving platter.

music to cook by The Beatles, *Sgt. Pepper's Lonely Hearts Club Band* is the ultimate psychedelic experience.

liquid assets The sweet bubbliness of pink (rosé) champagne is a great color complement and a perfect counterbalance for the bite of the wasabi.

bloody oyster shooters

Nothing kick-starts a Sunday brunch better than a freshly shucked oyster swimming in a shot of Bloody Caesar (a Bloody Mary made with Clamato juice) and topped with freshly grated horseradish.

1 cup Clamato juice or tomato juice, chilled

$1/2$ cup lemon vodka

2 tablespoons freshly squeezed lemon juice + 1 lemon wedge

$1/4$ teaspoon salt

$1/4$ teaspoon freshly ground black pepper

4 shakes Worcestershire sauce, or to taste

3 shakes Tabasco sauce, or to taste

2 tablespoons celery salt or regular salt

12 oysters, shucked

2 tablespoons freshly grated horseradish or $1/4–1/2$ teaspoon prepared horseradish

In a small pitcher, mix Clamato juice, vodka, lemon juice, salt, pepper, Worcestershire, and Tabasco. If fresh horseradish is not available, add prepared horseradish now.

Refrigerate for 1 hour.

Place celery salt on a small saucer $1/4$ inch deep. Moisten the rims of 12 shot glasses with the lemon wedge, then dip in salt.

Stir Caesar mix, then fill shot glasses $3/4$ full. Drop an oyster in each glass and sprinkle with fresh horseradish, if using. Say hello to the new day.

uncommon goods shot glasses; fresh horseradish; oysters

level of difficulty Once you open the oyster, the rest is a breeze.

active prep 25 minutes

inactive prep 1 hour

shortcuts Use preshucked oysters, available in jars. For best quality, purchase at fish stores.

advance work Bloody Caesar mix can be made up to 2 days in advance; oysters can be shucked and refrigerated in their own liquor up to a few hours in advance.

music to cook by Blue Öyster Cult, *Agents of Fortune* is the thinking man's heavy metal.

fish cakes

I guess my mother forgot to tell me not to play with my food. To this day I can't resist any opportunity to play culinary tricks that mess with my guests' sense of reality. This salmon cupcake with dill mashed potato icing confounds at first, then reveals its hand with sophisticated flavors that trump the illusion.

icing

2 medium russet potatoes, peeled and cut in quarters

1 cup stemmed fresh dill

1/2 cup olive oil

1/2 cup heavy cream, at room temperature

2 tablespoons butter, at room temperature

Salt

cakes

8 ounces skinless salmon, preferably wild, cut into 1/2-inch cubes

2 green onions, finely sliced

3 tablespoons red bell pepper, finely chopped

3 tablespoons bread crumbs or panko

1 egg, beaten

2 tablespoons sour cream

2 tablespoons freshly squeezed lemon juice

2 tablespoons finely chopped fresh Italian parsley

2 cloves garlic, finely chopped

1 jalapeño pepper, seeds discarded, minced

1/2 teaspoon salt

1/4 teaspoon freshly ground black pepper

Vegetable oil spray

continued

Steam potatoes over boiling water until tender to the poke of a fork.

In a mini food processor or blender, purée dill and olive oil. Reserve.

Use a ricer, food mill, or a standard-issue fork to mash potatoes. In a medium glass or metal bowl, blend the potatoes with cream, butter, salt, and half of the dill oil. Add remaining dill oil to taste, if desired. Reserve.

Preheat oven to 400°F.

To a food processor, add salmon, green onions, bell pepper, bread crumbs, egg, sour cream, lemon juice, parsley, garlic, jalapeño, salt, and pepper. Pulse 3 or 4 times. If you don't have a food processor, chop ingredients finer than indicated and blend in a bowl.

Line a mini muffin tin with 16 paper liners. Generously spray interior of liners with vegetable oil. Spoon salmon mixture into liners. Bake for 12 minutes. Remove cakes from tin immediately so that cakes do not continue to cook.

When you are ready to ice the cakes, reheat potatoes by covering the bowl with aluminum foil and placing it over a pot of boiling water for 5 minutes.

Ice cakes with mashed potatoes. Use the tines of a fork to shape icing.

uncommon goods mini muffin tin; mini muffin paper liners

the adventure club Divide the mashed potatoes into 3 batches. Color 1 batch as directed, 1 batch with some beet juice, and keep 1 batch white.

level of difficulty About the same as making cupcakes from scratch.

active prep 1 hour

cooking time 15 minutes

shortcuts Use instant mashed potatoes (with everything else going on, who's gonna know).

advance work Fish cake mixture can be prepped and mashed potatoes can be made earlier in the day.

multiplicity For each additional batch of fish cakes, make an additional half recipe of icing.

music to cook by John Lurie, *Fishing with John* showcases amusing music from the cable television series, and features Tom Waits.

liquid assets A Cru Beaujolais, sometimes considered the poor man's Burgundy, is a lively match for the bright flavors of this savory cupcake.

samurai scallops

Colorful and intricately decorated porcelain Chinese spoons can be found in practically any Chinatown dry goods store for about a buck each. And while you are in Chinatown, you can pick up the rest of the ingredients for about half of what they would cost in the Asian section of your grocery store (which is cheap to begin with). For a real adventure, stick around for lunch, and take your time, because your guests will think you spent all day creating the explosive flavors in this exotic tasting, but simple-to-make bite.

2 green onions, minced

2 tablespoons finely grated fresh ginger

2 garlic cloves, minced

2 tablespoons minced fresh cilantro

2 tablespoons seasoned rice vinegar

2 tablespoons toasted sesame oil

2 tablespoons soy sauce

3 tablespoons canola oil

1 tablespoon fresh squeezed lime juice

12 whole sea scallops (26–30 count; that's 26 to 30 to a pound) **or**
6 (13–15 count) **sea scallops cut in half like 2 half-moons**

Salt

Freshly ground black pepper

½ cup sesame seeds

In a small bowl, add green onions, ginger, garlic, cilantro, rice vinegar, sesame oil, soy sauce, 2 tablespoons of canola oil, and the lime juice. Whisk ingredients together. Reserve.

Remove the tough muscle from the side of each scallop if this has not already been done. Do not rinse scallops; their natural juices will help the sesame seeds stick. Season with salt and pepper.

Place sesame seeds on a plate. Pat down top and bottom sides of each scallop in sesame seeds. Reserve on a plate.

continued

In a sauté pan, over medium-high heat, add remaining tablespoon canola oil. When oil is hot, add scallops, placing them sesame-crusted-side down. Sear for approximately 1$\frac{1}{2}$ minutes, or until the sesame seeds on the bottom turn golden brown. To help maintain the bond between the seeds and the pan, avoid moving the pan. Turn and sear on other sesame-crusted side for 1 more minute.

To assemble, line up soup spoons for each bite. Place one teaspoon of vinaigrette in each spoon, and top with a scallop.

uncommon goods Chinese soup spoons

level of difficulty Infinitely easier than finding parking in Chinatown.

active prep 15 minutes

cooking time 5 minutes

shortcuts Replace the dipping sauce with a store-bought Asian vinaigrette.

advance work Vinaigrette can be made up to 2 days in advance.

music to cook by Various Artists, *Asian Travels* contains ambient mixes of contemporary Asian music, including cuts by Nusrat Fateh Ali Kahn and Euphoria.

liquid assets The big, lycheelike flavors of Gewürtzraminer are a natural pairing for Asian food in general and, in this particular case, with the ginger-soy vinaigrette and sesame-crusted scallops. You can also stick with the Asian theme and serve cold sake.

finger-lickin' shrimp

I owe this simple yet sophisticated recipe to my grilling guru, Elizabeth Karmel. Its genius rests in the fact that when you peel the salt-crusted shells off the shrimp, the salt residue on your fingers provides the perfect amount of seasoning for the sweet shrimp and aromatic dipping sauce. You'll have to put down your drink for this one—its finger-lickin' goodness requires both hands and a clean-up crew.

3/4 cup best-available olive oil

2 tablespoons freshly squeezed lemon juice

2 cloves garlic, minced

2 tablespoons minced fresh Italian parsley

2 teaspoons minced fresh oregano or thyme or 1 teaspoon dried

12 colossal shrimp (13–15 count; that's 13 to 15 to a pound), **shells on**

1/2 cup kosher salt or coarse sea salt

Preheat grill to medium-high heat.

In a small bowl, prepare dipping sauce by whisking together 1/2 cup of the olive oil, the lemon juice, garlic, parsley, and oregano. Reserve.

Using a paring knife, make a 1/4-inch incision down the backs of the shrimp. Devein them, but do not remove the shells.

In a medium bowl, add remaining 1/4 cup olive oil and the shrimp. Toss the shrimp in the oil, then sprinkle salt overtop, and toss thoroughly so that the shrimp are coated in salt.

Grill shrimp directly over the heat or pan cook for approximately 3 minutes per side, or until shrimp are opaque throughout. Serve with dipping sauce.

level of difficulty About as easy as bringing home a bucket of that other finger-lickin' food.

active prep 15 minutes

cooking time 10 minutes

shortcuts Use a store-bought dipping oil.

advance work Shrimp can be deveined (but not salted) up to a day in advance; dipping sauce actually improves if made hours in advance.

multiplicity For each additional batch of shrimp, make an additional half recipe of dipping sauce.

music to cook by The Rolling Stones, *Sticky Fingers* is a hedonistic classic.

liquid assets New Zealand is the new kid on the Sauvignon Blanc block. These wines are minerally and complex with the edge necessary to withstand the salt lickin' and the oil dippin'.

maple salmon suckers

Honey, I shrunk the entrée! This savory sucker is a bite-sized version of a maple-glazed, pepper-crusted salmon fillet that is one of the most requested entrées in my repertoire. Slicing the fillet into thin strips allows the maple-soy marinade to completely penetrate the fish, delivering a crowd-pleasing candied salmon that is so much greater than the sum of its parts.

1½ pounds salmon fillet, preferably wild (select thickest fillet available)

¾ cup maple syrup

¼ cup soy sauce

2 tablespoons coarsely grated black pepper

Slice salmon into ¼-inch-thick strips (see diagram).

Place salmon slices in a resealable plastic bag along with the syrup and soy. Force out the air and seal. Marinate in the refrigerator for a minimum of 4 hours, but ideally for 24 hours.

At the same time, soak 6-inch bamboo skewers in water (resealable plastic bags work well for this task too).

Preheat grill to high heat.

Remove salmon from marinade and skewer from the wide end.

Place pepper on a small plate and dip one edge of the salmon in it.

Grill salmon on a well-oiled BBQ grate over direct heat, or directly under a broiler for 1 minute per side, or until just cooked throughout, yet still moist. Serve immediately, or suffer the consequence of the fish drying out.

uncommon goods 6-inch bamboo skewers

level of difficulty All the hard work is being done for you by the marinade.

active prep 15 minutes

inactive prep 4–24 hours

cooking time 5 minutes

shortcuts In an imperfect world, you can marinate the salmon for as little as 15 minutes. This will glaze the fish with maple and soy instead of marinating it throughout.

advance work Fish can be cut and marinated up to a day in advance. It can be skewered and pepper-crusted a couple of hours before grilling. Cover tightly with plastic wrap to retain moistness.

multiplicity For each additional batch of salmon, make an additional third of the marinade.

music to cook by Lucinda Williams, *World Without Tears* is full of hard-hitting lyrics that aren't always sweet but call life like it is.

liquid assets Alsatian Riesling is a fruity wine with little residual sugar that will balance the mapley sweetness of the salmon.

margarita ceviche

yield: 12 bites

Ceviche is a refreshing Latin American delicacy consisting of raw fish or shellfish that is "cooked" by the acids in the lime juice in which it is marinated. As long as you have access to fresh fish or scallops, it's a breeze to make. My version is accented by a splash of tequila—another ingredient that results in an altered state when it comes into contact with lime juice.

14 aesthetically pleasing limes (2 are back-ups)

6 large sea scallops

2½ tablespoons olive oil

2 tablespoons freshly squeezed orange juice

2 tablespoons tequila

1 medium tomato, diced into tiny cubes

1 avocado, peeled, pitted, and diced into tiny cubes

½ cup stemmed fresh cilantro, finely chopped

¼ cup diced red onion

1 serrano chile, minced

Salt

3 cups rock salt (for presentation)

Slice the top third off the limes and use a juicer (ideally electric) or a reamer to juice both halves. Carefully preserve the shape of the larger lime shell halves when you juice them. Reserve the juice and the 12 best-looking large lime shells.

Use a small pair of scissors and melon baller or spoon to clip and scoop out as much of the lime membrane as possible from the shells. Run the shells on the juicer again to clean up the interiors. Freeze for 1 hour, or until completely frozen.

Dice scallops into ¼-inch cubes. Transfer to a medium bowl and add 1 cup of the lime juice. Toss thoroughly. Place bowl in fridge for ½ hour.

Strain off lime juice and discard. Reserve scallops.

In a medium bowl, whisk olive oil, 3 tablespoons lime juice, orange juice, and tequila. Add scallops, tomato, avocado, cilantro, onion, and chile. Toss thoroughly. Salt to taste.

Fill frozen lime shells with ceviche and set them in rock salt.

level of difficulty Hollowing out the limes requires the surgical skills of an ER wannabe. The rest is non-invasive.

active prep 1 hour

inactive prep 1 hour

shortcuts Serve ceviche in shot glasses or mini paper cups.

advance work Scallops should be cooked in lime juice no more than 4 hours before serving. Once they have been cooked, the rest of the ceviche can be assembled. At showtime, simply spoon into lime shells.

multiplicity For each additional batch of scallops, increase the lime juice in the cooking stage by half.

music to cook by Jimmy Buffett, *Meet Me in Margaritaville: The Ultimate Collection* is a disc that begs the question: Is it better to burn out than to waste away?

liquid assets What else? A classic margarita made with real lime juice.

vodka & latkes

They're not just for Chanukah anymore.

2 medium russet potatoes, peeled and grated

1 egg, beaten

1 tablespoon matzo meal

1 tablespoon minced onion

½ teaspoon salt

¼ cup canola oil for frying

1 bunch fresh dill, cherry-picked for 12 of the nicest tops

¼ cup sour cream

3 ounces smoked salmon

1½ cups lemon vodka, chilled in the freezer

uncommon goods shot glasses

level of difficulty As easy as making breakfast pancakes.

active prep 15 minutes

cooking time 10 minutes

shortcuts Serve open-faced with a dollop of sour cream, a piece of salmon, and a whisper of dill.

advance work Salmon can be portioned up to 2 days in advance. With some sacrifice to the crispiness, the latkes can be fried earlier in the day and reheated in a 450°F oven for 5 minutes just before the assembling stage.

music to cook by Leonard Cohen, *Ten New Songs* is a poignant disc from a golden voice (some say an acquired taste) that just keeps getting smoother.

Squeeze excess water out of potatoes. In a large bowl, toss potatoes with egg, matzo meal, onion, and salt.

In a large sauté pan over medium-high heat, add oil. When oil is hot, drop 12 one-teaspoon dollops of potatoes into oil and flatten gently with a fork. Fry for 2 minutes, or until the bottom side is golden brown and crispy. Flip and cook for 2 more minutes, or until the second side is crispy. Drain on a paper towel. Repeat the first part of the process with 12 more dollops. This time, after the bottoms are crispy, but before flipping the latkes, place a dill top on the uncooked top side of each latke. Using your finger, gently press dill into the potatoes. Flip latkes, then use a fork to press the latke down against the surface of the pan. Cook until the bottom side is crispy.

To assemble, line up the first batch of latkes. Top with a teaspoon of sour cream and a couple of layers of salmon. Cover with a dill-encrusted latke and serve with a shot of vodka. L'Chaim!

tuna fish & chips

Consider the lowly tortilla chip. Most of the time we take them for granted and eat them by the handful with salsa. But these triangular marvels of blue stone-ground corn are the perfect vehicle for a melt-in-your-mouth slice of cumin-crusted ahi tuna.

avocado relish

1 ripe but still firm avocado, diced into ¼-inch cubes

½ cup frozen corn kernels, thawed

¼ cup stemmed fresh cilantro leaves, finely chopped

¼ cup diced red onion

2 tablespoons freshly squeezed lime juice

Salt

Freshly ground black pepper

tuna

12 ounces ahi (or albacore) **tuna, 1 inch thick**

1 teaspoon ground cumin

1 teaspoon freshly ground black pepper

½ teaspoon ground coriander

½ teaspoon salt

¼ teaspoon cayenne pepper

1 tablespoon canola oil

12 cosmetically perfect blue corn tortilla chips

continued

In a medium bowl, combine all the relish ingredients and toss gently. Reserve.

 Using a long, sharp knife, cut tuna into triangular strips, 1¼ inches per side (see diagram).

In a small bowl, combine cumin, pepper, coriander, salt, and cayenne. Rub spice mixture generously on all 3 long sides of the tuna.

Heat a nonstick pan over high heat. When pan is smoking hot, add canola oil. Wait 10 seconds, then add tuna. Sear for 30 seconds per side, or until fish is cooked on the outside, but still rare in the center. Transfer to a plate. Slice into ½-inch-thick triangles.

To assemble, line up tortilla chips. Top each with a dollop of avocado relish and a slice of tuna.

level of difficulty The only challenge is staying focused for the 1½ minutes that the tuna is searing. If necessary, double up on your Ritalin.

active prep 30 minutes

cooking time 1½ minutes

shortcuts Skip the relish and put a thin slice of avocado between the tuna and the tortilla chip.

advance work With minimal sacrifice, tuna can be seared earlier in the day and served at room temperature. Slice just before serving. Relish can be made earlier in the day.

music to cook by David Bowie, *The Rise and Fall of Ziggy Stardust and the Spiders from Mars* is a glam manifesto that has no connection to this recipe but is always a trip.

liquid assets The chips, avocado relish, and cumin all beg for a Mexican beer or a margarita.

coconut shrimp lollypops

This is the one that started it all. Developing this recipe was the beginning of my love affair with small bites. The harmonic convergence of sweet fresh coconut, succulent shrimp, tropical dipping sauce, and a Trader Vic's–style presentation was an instant crowd-pleaser. Like a trained seal, I keep performing this trick so I can bask in the applause and enjoy the tasty treat I am rewarded with each time for my efforts.

apricot-ginger dipping sauce

- **¾ cup of apricot jam**
- **1 jalapeño pepper, seeds discarded, minced**
- **2 tablespoons seasoned rice vinegar or freshly squeezed lime juice**
- **1 tablespoon peeled and grated fresh ginger**
- **1 tablespoon Dijon mustard**

coconut shrimp lollypops

- **1 coconut, ideally prescored** (first-timers should buy a spare coconut)
- **½ cup beer**
- **1 cup all-purpose flour**
- **1 egg**
- **1 teaspoon cayenne pepper**
- **¾ teaspoon baking powder**
- **½ teaspoon salt**
- **12 jumbo shrimp** (21–25 count; that's 21 to 30 to a pound) **shelled and deveined**
- **3–5 cups peanut oil, or vegetable oil, for frying**
- **1 wedge of watermelon** (for presentation)

Place all dipping sauce ingredients in a blender or food processor. Purée. Reserve.

 With the coconut and a medium-size bowl in hand, go find yourself a concrete step. Break the coconut in half by banging the center (along the equator of the coconut) repeatedly on the edge of the step (see diagram). Split the coconut over the bowl and salvage some of the water if possible. Reserve the smaller half of

continued

the coconut. Bang the larger half on the concrete to break it into smaller pieces. Back in your kitchen, use a table knife to separate the coconut meat from the shell. Then use a vegetable peeler or paring knife to remove the brown skin from the meat.

 Using the fine part of your grater shred 2 cups of coconut. (Not all graters have grates that will work. For sanctioned grater surfaces, see diagram). Reserve in a shallow bowl.

Pour coconut water into a measuring cup and if necessary top off with beer until you have ¾ cup of liquid. Reserve. If you are using store-bought shredded coconut (and consequently do not have any coconut water), replace mixture with ¾ cup of beer.

In a large bowl, combine flour, coconut water/beer mixture, egg, cayenne, baking powder, and salt. Beat until it is smooth. Add a bit more flour or beer, if necessary, so that the batter has the consistency of thick pancake batter. Reserve.

 Use a paper towel to pat dry the shrimp. Tightly wrap each shrimp like a pinwheel (with the tail end of the shrimp on the outside), then place one shrimp on the end of each 6-inch bamboo skewer (see diagram). Reserve in refrigerator.

Pour oil into a small, tall pot until it is 3 inches deep. Heat oil until it reaches 350°F (see Fear of Frying, page 126).

While oil is heating, dip each shrimp in the batter, then pat it down in the coconut shreds so that the entire "lollypop" is covered in coconut shreds. Transfer to a plate.

When oil is ready, submerge 4 shrimp at a time into the oil. Don't worry if the skewers go into the oil. Fry for approximately 2 minutes, or until coconut is golden brown, rotating once or twice. Transfer lollypops to a paper towel.

Skim any wayward coconut shreds from the oil. Adjust heat so that it is 350°F again and continue with next batch. For a creative presentation, stick skewers in a watermelon wedge and/or serve the dipping sauce in the unused coconut half.

uncommon goods 6-inch bamboo skewers; a whole coconut.

level of difficulty Like learning how to line dance. If you attempt all of the steps together, it can be intimidating the first time around. But if you tackle each of the four individual steps of this recipe one at a time, they are a cinch to master.

active prep 1 hour

cooking time 20 minutes

shortcuts Skip the whole coconut deal. Use store-bought unsweetened shredded coconut in place of the fresh coconut, beer in place of the coconut water, and a small decorative bowl for the dipping sauce in place of the coconut shell.

advance work Coconut can be grated, shrimp can be skewered, and the dipping sauce and batter can all be made earlier in the day. The shrimp can be battered and dredged a couple of hours before serving and refrigerated on a plate. That just leaves the deep-frying to be done at showtime.

music to cook by Harry Nilsson, *Everybody's Talking*—"she put de lime in de coconut, drink 'em bot' togeder . . ."

liquid assets A crisp semidry German or Alsace Reisling has the acidity to cut through the deep-fried coconut and the fruitiness to temper the heat of the dipping sauce.

meat

gaucho snacks, page 42

gaucho snacks

yield: 16 bites

Argentineans use chimichurri sauce as a marinade and a condiment for simply grilled meats, poultry, and fish. You can buy it in a jar, but the stabilization process renders it a pale reflection of the original. Once you taste this complex, brightly flavored, homemade version, you will want to slather it on everything from your morning toast to your lover's toes.

chimichurri sauce

2 cups stemmed fresh parsley, ideally Italian flat-leaf

5 tablespoons olive or vegetable oil

3 tablespoons freshly squeezed lemon juice

3–5 cloves garlic, minced

1 medium shallot, minced, or 2 tablespoons minced onion

2 tablespoons sherry wine vinegar or red wine vinegar

1 teaspoon red pepper flakes

1/2 teaspoon salt

1/2 teaspoon freshly ground black pepper

gaucho steak

3 tablespoons salt

1 tablespoon cayenne pepper

Two 1-pound New York strip steaks, ideally 1 1/4 inches thick

1 sourdough baguette, sliced into sixteen 1/4-inch-thick slices

Place all chimichurri ingredients in a food processor or blender and purée. Reserve.

Preheat grill to high heat.

In a small bowl, mix salt and cayenne. Rub mixture into both sides of the steak.

Place the steaks over direct heat and grill to desired degree of doneness (approximately 6 minutes per side for medium-rare). Remove the steaks from the grill, cover with aluminum foil, and let rest for 5 minutes. If you do not have a grill (or it is under 3 feet of snow), eliminate the cayenne pepper from the dry rub, and cook steaks in a heavy pan over medium-high heat for approximately 6 minutes per side.

To assemble, slice steaks into 1/4-inch-thick pieces. Set pieces on baguette slices and top with chimichurri sauce.

level of difficulty Requires basic caveman skills.

active prep 20 minutes

cooking time 20 minutes

shortcuts Skip the sauce. Even without it, this is a killer bite for steak lovers.

advance work Chimichurri sauce can be made up to a day in advance. With minimal sacrifice, steak can be grilled up to a day in advance and served at room temperature. Slice just before serving.

music to cook by Steely Dan, *Gaucho* is a time capsule from the era of pop fusion.

liquid assets An Argentinean Malbec, big and rough just like the gauchos, will wrangle the bold flavors of the chimichurri sauce and the steak.

chorizo corn pups

As the old joke goes, there are three foods to be found at a state fair. Fried food, food on a stick, and fried food on a stick. My philosophy is that if you are going to eat fried food on a stick, make every calorie count. That's why I've downsized the portion and upgraded the dog.

1/2 cup flour

1/2 cup cornmeal

1/2 tablespoon sugar

1/2 tablespoon baking powder

1/2 teaspoon salt

1/2 teaspoon chili powder

1 egg

1/2 cup milk

2 tablespoons canola, or other vegetable oil

3–4 cups peanut oil, for frying

8 inches of chorizo (andouille sausage is a good second choice), **ideally 1 inch in diameter**

assortment of mustards (e.g., Dijon, honey mustard, grainy country-style, ballpark)

In a large bowl, mix flour, cornmeal, sugar, baking powder, salt, and chili powder.

In a medium-sized bowl, mix egg, milk, and canola oil.

Slowly pour liquid ingredients into the bowl of dry ingredients and whisk until the batter is smooth. It should be the thickness of pancake batter.

Pour peanut oil into a small, tall pot until it is 3 inches deep. Heat oil until it reaches 350°F (see Fear of Frying, page 126).

Peel and discard chorizo casing and cut sausage into 1/2-inch slices.

Place each chorizo slice on a 6-inch bamboo skewer, then dip in batter. Fry 6 puppies at a time for approximately 1 1/2 minutes, or until batter turns golden brown, rotating once during frying. Transfer puppies to a paper towel. Serve with an assortment of mustards set out in small bowls.

uncommon goods 6-inch bamboo skewers

level of difficulty Look at it this way: It doesn't take a PhD to make corn dogs at the fair.

active prep 20 minutes

cooking time 5 minutes

shortcuts Skip the skewers and serve as Chorizo Corn Puffs.

advance work Batter can be mixed, and sausage prepped and skewered, earlier in the day. At showtime, just dip sausages in batter and fry.

music to cook by Calexico, *Feast of Wire* is a marriage of traditional Mexican mariachi music and toe-tapping cinematic rock.

liquid assets Any light-bodied Mexican beer with a squirt of lime will be an effervescent foil for the crispy corn batter and spicy chorizo.

cocktail dates

In their unadorned state, dried Medjool dates are intense candy bombs that explode in your mouth with sweetness and richness. But stuff them with the nuttiness of Parmigiano-Reggiano, wrap them in the smoky saltiness of bacon, and bake them, and they will turn into molten balls of decadence that will blow your mind.

12 large dried Medjool dates

4-ounce chunk Italian Parmigiano-Reggiano cheese

6 slices bacon, cut in half widthwise

Preheat oven to 350°F.

Insert a bamboo skewer or a similar facsimile in the bottom of the date until the pointy tip rests on the bottom of the pit. Push the pit out of the stem side. Reserve dates.

Using your sharpest knife, cut Parmigiano-Reggiano into 1/4-inch slices. Cut those slices into 1/4-x-1-inch pieces (the resulting 1-inch pieces should be approximately the same diameter as a pencil). Cut the tip of each piece at a 45-degree angle.

Leading with the pointy end, stuff a stick of Parmigiano-Reggiano into the pit hole of each date.

Wrap each date with a slice of bacon. Set dates on a baking sheet, seam-sides down, and skewer each with a toothpick to hold bacon in place.

Bake for approximately 20 minutes, or until bacon is crispy. Caution: These flavor bombs are like molten lava when they come out of the oven. Let cool for a few minutes before serving.

uncommon goods Medjool dates or any other dried date (usually available in Mediterranean stores and specialty food stores); ungrated Parmigiano-Reggiano

the adventure club Use a cob-smoked or other specialty bacon.

level of difficulty If you have ever rolled a joint (or seen someone roll a joint . . . on TV), you are fully qualified.

active prep 25 minutes

cooking time 20 minutes

shortcuts Buy pitted dates.

advance work Dates can be stuffed and wrapped up to 24 hours in advance.

music to cook by Various Artists, *Cocktail Mix, Vol. 4: Soundtracks with a Twist* is a swingin' extravaganza of six-ties movie music, including tunes by Bacharach, Mancini, and Morricone.

liquid assets The over-the-top pruney qualities of an Italian Amarone are a good match for the naturally concen-trated sugars in the dates.

nest eggs

I get so excited when I am assembling these delicate nests. For me, the classic French salad served in a crispy potato basket is a perfect marriage of flavors and aesthetics. When I see them sitting on a dinner plate I can't help but look at them with a sense of wonder. The quail eggs may be challenging to find and the nests will definitely require some practice, but harmony like this doesn't come easy.

1 tablespoon olive oil

4 strips thick-cut bacon, sliced crosswise into ¼-inch strips

1 tablespoon red wine vinegar

1 teaspoon Dijon mustard

2 large russet potatoes, peeled

2 teaspoons cornstarch

4–5 cups peanut oil for frying

1 head frisée lettuce, cored, and chopped into ¼-inch pieces

Salt

Freshly ground black pepper

16 quail eggs (6 of these are back-ups), **cold**

In a sauté pan over medium-high heat, add olive oil and bacon. Cook bacon until just before it gets to the crispy stage. Using a slotted spoon, remove and reserve bacon. Remove pan from the heat and add vinegar. Stir to loosen up all the bacon bits, then stir in mustard. Transfer dressing to a medium bowl and reserve.

Shred potatoes on the coarse side of a grater. Squeeze out moisture from potatoes, then dry in paper towels. In a medium bowl, add potatoes and cornstarch. Toss thoroughly.

In a tall, medium pot, add oil until it is 3 inches deep. Heat oil to 350°F (see Fear of Frying, page 126).

continued

Dip a 3-inch round strainer in oil, then line the strainer all the way to the top with a 3/16-inch-thick layer of potato. Use a second 3-inch round strainer to hold potato in place. Deep fry for approximately 3 minutes or until golden. Twist top strainer to remove, then knock bottom strainer upside down on a hard surface to loosen nest. Repeat with all 12 nests. Drain on paper towels and reserve.

In a medium pot, bring 6 cups of water to a boil, then reduce to a simmer.

Just before you are about to boil the eggs, add lettuce and bacon to the bowl containing the dressing. Season with salt and pepper and toss.

Add eggs to the water and simmer for exactly 2 minutes and 15 seconds. Remove eggs with a slotted spoon and immediately run under cold water for 15 seconds. Tap shells lightly against a hard surface to break, and peel under warm water.

To assemble, line up potato nests, fill with frisée salad, and top each with a quail egg.

uncommon goods two 3-inch round strainers (about $2 each at most kitchen stores); quail eggs (available in Chinese markets, some specialty stores, and farmers' markets)

the adventure club Serve quail eggs in their (beautiful, speckled) shells, and let your guests peel them.

level of difficulty Like making origami; it's hard at first, then easy to duplicate.

active prep 1 hour 30 minutes

cooking time 40 minutes

shortcuts Use a store-bought vinaigrette.

advance work Bacon and dressing can be prepared earlier in the day; potato nests can be fried earlier in the day and reheated in a 450°F oven for 4 minutes. At showtime, boil the eggs, toss the salad, and assemble.

music to cook by Rufus Wainwright, *Rufus Wainwright* is the brilliant debut by the talented offspring from the nest of folk icons Kate McGarrigle and Loudon Wainwright III.

liquid assets A crisp dry white Bordeaux Graves or Pessac-Léognan will cut through the fattiness of the bacon dressing and the fried potato basket, and round out the bitterness of the frisée lettuce.

cowboy cookies

Sugar and spice and meat that's high-priced, that's what Cowboy Cookies are made of. Trust me, once you have tasted this slice of tenderloin, sandwiched between caramelized yams and slathered in smokiness, you'll know it was worth every penny.

chipotle aioli

- **2 cloves garlic, minced**
- **1 egg yolk, room temperature**
- **1/2 tablespoon freshly squeezed lemon juice**
- **1/8 teaspoon salt**
- **1/8 teaspoon freshly ground black pepper**
- **1/2 cup olive oil**
- **1 teaspoon chipotle chili powder or 1 tablespoon puréed canned chipotle in adobo sauce**

cookies

- **6 skinny yams or sweet potatoes** (about 2 inches in diameter) **or fatter ones if unavailable**
- **3 tablespoons olive oil**
- **4 teaspoons salt**
- **3 tablespoons New Mexican** (or any other pure) **chili powder**
- **2 tablespoons sugar**
- **1 tablespoon freshly ground black pepper**
- **Three 6-ounce filet mignons, 2 inches thick** (ask your butcher to cut these for you from the thin end of the tenderloin). **Alternatively, you can use a whole 1-pound pork tenderloin.**
- **1/4–1/2 cup of your favorite BBQ sauce**
- **1/4 cup chipotle aioli** (optional)

Preheat oven to 325°F.

Add the garlic, egg yolk, lemon juice, salt, and pepper to a blender or mini food processor and purée until smooth. Alternatively, whisk the ingredients together in a medium bowl.

continued

Very slowly drizzle in the oil with the motor running and purée until aioli thickens (should take 2–3 minutes). If you are using a whisk, keep whisking while slowly drizzling in the oil until the aioli is thick. Stir in chipotle. Reserve.

Place yams on their sides. With your sharpest knife, cut into ⅜-inch-thick slices. If yams are more than 2 inches (or so) in diameter, use a 2-inch round cookie cutter or a paring knife to trim to desired size.

In a medium bowl, add olive oil. Toss yam slices until they are lightly coated with oil. Sprinkle with 1 teaspoon salt. Spread on a nonstick baking sheet or on any parchment paper–lined sheet pan and bake for 30 minutes. Turn yams over and bake for 30 more minutes, or until yams are browned, slightly condensed, and begging to be eaten. Reserve in aluminum foil to keep warm.

Preheat grill to high heat.

While yams are baking, in a medium bowl, combine chili powder, sugar, and pepper. Generously rub down the filets with this dry rub. Wrap filets in wax paper or plastic wrap and let stand at room temperature for 30 minutes.

Just before grilling, pat down filets with remaining 3 teaspoons salt. Over direct heat, sear meat for 2 minutes a side on all 6 sides. Transfer to indirect heat, cover grill, and cook for approximately 6 more minutes for medium-rare, or until filets have reached your desired degree of doneness. Alternatively, filets can be broiled for approximately 10 minutes per side.

Place meat on a plate and cover with aluminum foil. Let rest for 5 minutes before slicing. Set each filet on its side and cut into ¼-inch-thick round slices.

To assemble, set out 2 rows of 12 yam slices each. Spoon ½ teaspoon BBQ sauce over each slice in the front row and ½ teaspoon chipotle aioli over each in the back row (if you don't make the aioli, replace with BBQ sauce). Top each yam in the first row with a slice of steak and cover with an aioli-slathered yam slice.

uncommon goods custom-cut beef tenderloin

level of difficulty Like making a club sandwich from scratch.

active prep 45 minutes

inactive prep 35 minutes

cooking time 1 hour 30 minutes

shortcuts Serve the steak between baguette slices.

advance work With minimal sacrifice, beef can be grilled up to a day in advance and served at room temperature. Slice just before serving. Yams can be made earlier in the day, then reheated in a 450°F oven for 5 minutes.

music to cook by Various Artists, *American Cowboy Songs* is a compilation of classic cowboy tunes—whoopie ti-yi-yo!

liquid assets Any self-respecting cowboy would chase this bite with a shot of bourbon. City slickers should head straight for a big California Cabernet or a spicy Zinfandel.

hog heaven

One man's cold cut is another man's charcuterie. This upscale baloney sandwich tastes far more sophisticated than it looks. And it will save your bacon by freeing you up to focus on more time- and preparation-intensive dishes.

⅓ cup grainy country-style mustard

3 tablespoons honey

1 teaspoon freshly ground black pepper

12 slices country-style white bread or any sandwich bread (Each slice may yield 2 bites depending on the size of the loaf and the cookie cutter.)

1 pound mortadella (an Italian salami), sliced 3/16 inch thick

In a small bowl, blend mustard, honey, and pepper.

Toast bread lightly, then spread with mustard, and top with mortadella. Use a pig-shaped cookie cutter to press out forms. Snack on the spoilin's.

uncommon goods pig-shaped cookie cutter

level of difficulty Child's play.

active prep 10 minutes

shortcuts This is a shortcut!

advance work Crostini should be assembled as close to serving time as possible to maintain the crispness of the toast.

music to cook by Various Artists, *O Brother, Where Art Thou?* soundtrack is a swell tribute to traditional American music.

liquid assets A full-bodied microbrew will send you to hog heaven.

inside-out BLTs*

If you want to see an object from a completely different perspective, look at it in a mirror. If you want to hear a song with fresh ears, listen to it over the telephone. And if you want to taste an old favorite in a whole new way, turn it inside out.

8 strips premium bacon, sliced crosswise into ⅛-inch strips

8 firm Roma tomatoes or green (unripe) tomatoes, cut into ¼-inch slices

1 cup flour

3 eggs, beaten

2 cups bread crumbs or panko

3 or more tablespoons olive oil

Salt

Freshly ground black pepper

4-ounce log goat cheese, approximately 1½ inches in diameter, sliced ⅛ inch thick

24 arugula leaves, lower stems discarded

Cook bacon over medium heat until crispy. Drain on a paper towel.

Select the 24 most uniform tomato slices and save the rest for tomorrow's lunch. Dredge slices in flour, then in eggs, then pat down in bread crumbs. Reserve on plates, but do not stack.

In a sauté pan over medium-high heat, add 3 tablespoons oil. When oil is hot, add as many breaded tomato slices as the pan can accommodate without them touching. Fry for approximately 2 minutes per side, or until browned and crispy. Remove from pan and drain on paper towels. Add more oil if necessary for subsequent batches.

To assemble, line up 12 fried tomato slices. Season with salt and pepper, then top each with 1 cheese slice, a mound of bacon shrapnel, and 2 arugula leaves. Cover with a second fried tomato slice. Secure with a toothpick. Let cool for a minute before serving. (Tomatoes have a surprising ability to hold the heat.)

*OK, technically it's not a BLT, but the goat cheese adds so much flavor and texture I couldn't resist. So sue me.

uncommon goods toothpicks with frilly tops

level of difficulty Requires the skill of an entry-level short-order cook.

active prep 30 minutes

cooking time 20 minutes

shortcuts Skip the bacon and arugula and make it an inside-out grilled cheese.

advance work Bacon, arugula, and cheese can all be prepped earlier in the day; tomatoes can be breaded, then refrigerated on a plate a couple of hours in advance. At showtime, simply fry the tomatoes and assemble the sandwiches.

music to cook by Yo La Tengo, *And Then Nothing Turned Itself Inside-Out* is literate pop from the Hoboken husband-and-wife duo.

liquid assets A white Rhône blend or a white Châteauneuf-du-Pape are lively, aromatic wines with the complexity necessary to match the multiple personalities of the ingredients in this bite.

fowl

chicken popsicles, page 60

chicken popsicles

yield: 12 popsicles

Chicken tenders, as their name suggests, are the tenderloin (a.k.a. filet mignon) of the poultry world. Most grocery stores now package them on their own for just a couple of dollars a pound more than boneless breasts. The crispy breaded crust and succulent interior make these easy lemon-glazed chicken popsicles a truly grown-up treat.

6 chicken tenders

Salt

Freshly ground black pepper

²/₃ cup flour

2 eggs, beaten

²/₃ cup panko or coarse bread crumbs

¹/₃ cup grated Parmigiano-Reggiano cheese

2 tablespoons Mrs. Dash Italian blend or 1 tablespoon dried oregano + 1 tablespoon dried thyme

2 tablespoons butter

3 tablespoons freshly squeezed lemon juice

1 pineapple (for presentation)

Chicken tenders contain a thin white tendon that runs the length of the tender. These can be eaten but are stringy when cooked. To remove the tendon, pinch its protruding tip between the blade of a paring knife and your thumb. Using your other hand, grasp the tendon just below the blade between your thumbnail and pointer finger, and pull down against the meat (see diagram).

Cut each tender in half horizontally, creating 2 pieces that should be approximately 1 x 2 inches. Season with salt and pepper.

Set out 3 medium bowls. Place flour in one, eggs in the second, and panko, Parmesan, and Italian spices in the third. Line the 3 bowls in a row.

Roll tenders in flour until well covered, then dip in egg until well soaked, and finally, roll in bread crumb mixture until completely covered. Transfer to a plate.

In a frying pan, over medium-high heat, melt butter. Add tenders when butter begins to sizzle. Cook for approximately 3 minutes on the first side, or until golden brown. Turn once and cook for approximately 2 more minutes, or until the second side is golden brown and the tenders are cooked throughout. To test for doneness, make a small incision in a sacrificial tender. If any pink remains, return to heat for another minute or two.

Transfer tenders to a plate. Remove pan from heat and add lemon juice. Stir for a few seconds to loosen up brown bits and let the lemon juice reduce. Drizzle a few drops over each tender and season with salt.

Place each chicken tender on a 6-inch bamboo skewer, then stick skewers in pineapple.

uncommon goods 6-inch bamboo skewers; panko (Japanese bread crumbs, available in Japanese groceries and some grocery stores)

level of difficulty Think Shake 'N Bake.

active prep 20 minutes

cooking time 10 minutes

shortcuts Buy Italian-style bread crumbs that are seasoned with herbs and cheese.

advance work Tenders can be breaded earlier in the day and refrigerated on a plate.

multiplicity For each additional batch of popsicles, make an additional quarter recipe of the bread crumb mixture.

music to cook by Ry Cooder, *Chicken Skin Music.* Any excuse to put on a Ry Cooder album is a good excuse.

liquid assets A crisp Italian Soave will cut through the rich crust and match the acidity of the lemon glaze.

fois gras & jam

This combination of rich foie gras pâté and savory strawberry compote is peanut butter & jam for consenting (and discriminating) adults.

1 tablespoon canola oil

3 shallots, minced

1$\frac{1}{2}$ cups fresh strawberries, hulled and quartered, or frozen unsweetened strawberries

1 teaspoon salt

2 tablespoons balsamic vinegar

$\frac{1}{2}$ teaspoon freshly ground black pepper

6 slices egg bread or white bread

8 ounces foie gras or goose or duck liver pâté, trimmed of any gelatin or peppercorns, at room temperature

Preheat oven to 250°F.

In a sauté pan over medium-high heat, add oil and shallots. Sauté for 3 minutes, or until shallots start becoming translucent. Add strawberries and salt and continue cooking for 5 minutes, or until strawberries begin to soften and break down. Add vinegar and pepper and cook for another 2 minutes. Let cool.

Toast bread in the oven for 10 minutes or until it begins to crisp up, but before it gets to the stage of browning.

Make a traditional PB&J sandwich using a thick layer of pâté in place of peanut butter and a thin layer of strawberry compote as the jam (about 3 parts pâté to 1 part compote). Trim crusts and cut in triangles.

uncommon goods foie gras, goose or duck liver pâté

level of difficulty Like making a kid breakfast and throwing together a sandwich for lunch at the same time.

active prep 30 minutes

cooking time 20 minutes

shortcuts Use an unsweetened dark berry jam in place of the homemade strawberry compote.

advance work Strawberry compote can be made up to 2 days in advance. Sandwich should be assembled as close to serving time as possible to maintain the crispness of the toast.

music to cook by Elton John, *Madman Across the Water* is Elton in his prime.

liquid assets Foie gras without Sauternes is like peanut butter without jam. To complete the trompe l'oeil, serve it in apple juice glasses.

chinese snow cones

yield: 12 bites

Chinese chicken salad is an Asian-inspired California creation consisting of grilled chicken, crisp lettuce, deep-fried wonton strips, and nuts, all tossed in a tangy ginger vinaigrette. Everybody's version is different. With most, you can eat the wontons out of the crispy, crunchy salad. Mine is reengineered so that you can eat the salad out of the crispy, crunchy wonton.

1 large single boneless, skinless chicken breast

Salt

1$\frac{1}{4}$ cups peanut oil

Sixteen 3$\frac{1}{2}$-inch square wonton wrappers (4 are back-ups)

1 tablespoon freshly squeezed lime juice

1 tablespoon peeled and finely grated fresh ginger

1 tablespoon honey

1 teaspoon Dijon mustard

1 teaspoon soy sauce

1 teaspoon seasoned rice vinegar

2 cups sliced and finely diced Napa cabbage (about $\frac{1}{2}$ head)

1 cup sliced and finely diced radicchio (about $\frac{1}{2}$ head)

$\frac{1}{2}$ cup coarsely chopped roasted unsalted cashews

$\frac{1}{3}$ cup canned mandarin slices chopped

$\frac{1}{4}$ cup stemmed and finely sliced fresh cilantro

2 green onions, finely sliced

Red pepper flakes

continued

Season chicken breast with salt. In a small sauté pan over medium-high heat, add 1 tablespoon peanut oil. Cover and cook chicken for 6 minutes per side, or until no pink remains. Reserve.

Preheat oven to 350°F. In a small bowl, set out 1 cup peanut oil along with a small pastry brush. On a baking sheet, set out 12 paper cones and double them up (one on top of the other) with an additional 12 cones.

Trim 12 wonton wrappers according to diagram. Brush both sides of each wrapper with peanut oil. Wrap 1 wrapper around each cone (see diagram) and press seams together. Twist the bottom to a point. Bake for 7 minutes, or until golden brown and crispy. When cones cool, twist them off the cups and reserve.

Dice chicken finely. Reserve.

In a large bowl, whisk together remaining 3 tablespoons peanut oil, lime juice, ginger, honey, mustard, soy sauce, and vinegar. Just before serving, add chicken along with cabbage, radicchio, cashews, mandarins, cilantro, and green onions. Toss thoroughly and season to taste with salt and red pepper flakes. Serve in wonton cones.

uncommon goods cone-shaped paper cups (liberate them from the nearest office water cooler or visit a party supply store); wonton wrappers (available in Asian groceries and the refrigerated section of many grocery stores)

the adventure club Replace chicken with duck, shrimp, or tuna.

level of difficulty Wonton cups require the pattern-making skills and dexterity of an amateur seamstress.

active prep 1 hour

cooking time 20 minutes

shortcuts Skip the wonton cups and serve chicken salad in paper cones or mini paper cups; start with a precooked chicken breast.

advance work Wonton cones, ginger dressing, and the slicing and dicing of salad ingredients can be done up to a day in advance. Toss just before serving.

music to cook by Kazu Matsui, *Sign of the Snow Crane* is a great collection of the traditional Japanese bamboo flute music known as *shakuhachi*.

liquid assets A Kabinett Riesling from Germany, or a New World off-dry Riesling should supply the perfect balance of crispness and fruitiness for the vibrant flavors of the salad and the zingy dressing.

lucky duck

I love to serve these as the headliner when I am staging an evening of bites. Duck is a rare treat that most people only encounter on restaurant menus, but there is no reason not to serve it at home. True, whole ducks can be intimidating to prepare, but individually packaged breasts are a snap once you understand how they perform. The intensity of the duck, the savory plum sauce, and the crispy wontons make these a showstopper, so plan on two bites per guest.

1 cup peanut oil, for frying

Six 3½-inch square wonton wrappers, sliced diagonally into 2 triangles

One 14-ounce boneless duck breast, ideally Muscovy duck

1 teaspoon salt

2 shallots, minced

2 tablespoons balsamic vinegar

⅓ cup plum jam

2 tablespoons Grand Marnier

1 tablespoon peeled and finely grated or minced fresh ginger

1 teaspoon coarsely ground black pepper

2 green onions, thinly sliced on the bias, for garnish

Preheat oven to 350°F.

Pour oil into a small pot until it is 1 inch deep. Heat oil until it reaches 350°F (see Fear of Frying, page 126). Add 1 wonton skin. Fry for approximately 10 seconds, or until light gold. Turn and fry for 5–10 more seconds, until second side is light gold. Remove and place on paper towel. Repeat with remaining wontons. Reserve.

Place the duck skin-side up. Using a sharp knife, score six ¼-inch-deep cuts across the skin at a 45-degree angle. Season both sides of each duck breast with salt.

Heat a well-seasoned skillet or nonstick pan over medium-high heat. When pan is hot, add duck, skin-side down, and cook for 5 minutes, or until skin is brown

continued

fowl   67

and crispy. Flip and cook for 2 more minutes. If you are unfamiliar with duck breasts, don't be put off by their unusual look. The fat-to-meat proportions reverse themselves when cooked, as much of the fat is rendered and the meat expands.

Remove pan from heat (save the drippings) and transfer duck, skin-side up, to a baking sheet. Bake for 6 minutes for medium-rare, or until cooked to desired degree of doneness.

While duck is baking, carefully discard all but two tablespoons of the duck drippings from the skillet (culinary hedonists should refrigerate the duck fat in an air-tight container and fry your eggs in it for breakfast). Return pan to medium heat and add shallots. Stir occasionally for 2 minutes, or until shallots begin to turn golden. Add vinegar to the pan and stir with a wooden spoon to loosen up the browned bits left by the duck. Add jam, Grand Marnier, ginger, and pepper, and cook, stirring occasionally, for 3 minutes. Remove from heat.

Remove duck from oven, cover with aluminum foil, and let it rest for 5 minutes. Slice on the diagonal into 3/16-inch-thick slices.

To assemble, line up wontons and place one duck slice overtop. Top with a dollop of the plum compote and a slice of green onion.

uncommon goods Muscovy duck breast (often kept in the frozen meat section of the grocery store); wonton wrappers (available in Asian groceries and the refrigerated section of many grocery stores)

level of difficulty Like driving a new car for the first time. Once you get familiar with how the duck handles, you will quickly be in control.

active prep 25 minutes

cooking time 20 minutes

shortcuts Skip the plum compote and top the duck with a tiny dollop of ginger marmalade or mango chutney.

advance work Duck, compote, and wontons can all be prepared up to a day in advance and brought to room temperature just before serving. Slice duck breast just before serving.

music to cook by Various Artists, *The Quintet: Jazz at Massey Hall* is one of the most famous live recordings in the history of jazz, bringing together five of bebop's greatest figures: Dizzie Gillespie, Bud Powell, Max Roach, Charlie Mingus, and Charlie Parker (who was actually billed as Charlie Chan in an effort to sidestep an exclusive recording contract).

liquid assets A Californian or Rhône Syrah will match the gaminess of the duck and dance with the sugary plum compote.

goose mousse

When you are preparing a flight of bites, it is always nice to have a few get-out-of-jail-free cards up your sleeve to buy some time for your more complicated recipes. This playful spin on the classic hors d'oeuvre will help you keep the bar high while leaving you plenty of time for your pièce de resistance.

12 slices bread, ideally an egg bread, challah, or brioche, but even Wonder Bread will do (Each slice may yield 2 or more bites depending on the size of the loaf and the cookie cutter.)

1 pound goose or duck liver pâté, trimmed of any gelatin or peppercorns, at room temperature

Toast bread. Spread a 3/16-inch-thick layer of pâté on each slice of toast. Use a duck- or goose-shaped cookie cutter to press out forms. Either recapture the pâté from the discarded pieces, or reward your efforts by feasting on the spoilin's.

uncommon goods duck- or goose-shaped cookie cutter

level of difficulty Child's play.

active prep 10 minutes

shortcuts It just doesn't get any shorter.

advance work Your gaggle of geese should be assembled as close to serving time as possible to maintain the crispness of the toast.

music to cook by Radiohead, *Hail to the Thief* is cryptic at times, crystal clear at others. Put "Sail to the Moon" on repeat.

liquid assets Red Rhônes, known for their gaminess, will play well with the goose liver pâté.

bang-bang drummettes

yield: 18 bites

Buffalo chicken wings (ordered "suicide" on the spice scale) used to be one of my guilty pleasures. But after countless baskets of mouth-scorching wings, my palate craves more complexity than Louisiana hot sauce and butter can deliver. My bang-bang marinade packs plenty of heat, but it also delivers multiple layers of sweetness and spice. And by using just the meatiest section of the wing, there is less fight and more bite. (See photograph on page 2.)

18 chicken wing drummettes

6 cloves garlic, minced

¼ cup pineapple juice

¼ cup soy sauce

2 tablespoons toasted sesame oil

2 tablespoons olive oil

2 tablespoons freshly squeezed lime juice

2 tablespoons honey

1 habanero or scotch bonnet chile, seeds discarded, minced, or 1 teaspoon habanero or scotch bonnet sauce

1 tablespoon ground cinnamon

If wings come attached with middle and/or tip sections, cut away the wings at the joint and save for soup.

Using a paring knife, cut around the bone just below the knuckle, at the skinny end of each drummette. Slice through the meat and tendon (see diagram). Scrape the meat up toward the fat end of the drummette, creating a ball-like shape at that end. (There is no need to be precise; the cooking process will complete your artistry.) Trim off the bit of fat at the knuckle. Transfer chicken to a large resealable plastic bag. Reserve.

In a blender, purée all remaining ingredients. Transfer marinade to the bag-o-chicken, force out the air, and seal. Refrigerate for a minimum of 2 hours, but ideally for 6 hours, massaging occasionally.

Preheat grill to medium-high heat.

Grill over direct heat for 20 minutes, rotating $1/4$ turn every 5 minutes, or until cooked throughout. Or bake in a 450°F oven for 25 minutes, ideally on a wire rack, turning once.

uncommon goods habanero chile or habanero sauce

level of difficulty Like a trip to the hairdresser: A few snips, a little fussing with some product, a bit of time for everything to settle into place—and you're good to go.

active prep 25 minutes

inactive prep 2–6 hours

cooking time 25 minutes

shortcuts Have your butcher trim and prep the wings.

advance work Drummettes can be prepared and left to marinate up to 24 hours in advance. With minimal sacrifice, they can also be cooked a few hours in advance, then reheated in a 450°F oven for 8 minutes.

multiplicity For each additional batch of drummettes, make an additional half recipe of the marinade.

music to cook by Moby, *Play* is full of evocative, melancholy, techno beats.

liquid assets A Belgian blonde beer has the rich flavor and aroma necessary to tame the habanero and temper the cinnamon.

veggies

caesar teaser, page 76

caesar teaser

The key to a Caesar salad is freshly grated Parmigiano-Reggiano. I should know. Since I made my first Caesar twenty years ago, I have made squillions of them. I'm so obsessed that I carry my well-worn salad bowl with me in a snare drum case when I take my show on the road. In this miniature incarnation, the cheese plays a new, but equally important, role. And talk about your childhood wishes—you can even eat the dishes!

parmesan cups

5-ounce block Parmigiano-Reggiano cheese, finely grated
(about 2 cups; inferior Parmesans may not be up to the task at hand.)

caesar

¼ cup safflower, canola, or olive oil

3 cloves garlic, minced

1½ tablespoons freshly squeezed lemon juice

2 teaspoons Dijon mustard

2 teaspoons red wine vinegar

2 anchovies or 1 teaspoon anchovy paste (omit if serving vegetarians)

1 teaspoon Worcestershire sauce

½ teaspoon salt

½ teaspoon coarsely ground black pepper

1 egg yolk, coddled (see page 127)

3 cups diced romaine lettuce hearts (the inner half of the romaine)

12 small croutons

Preheat oven to 350°F. Set out 4 shot glasses and turn them upside down.

On a nonstick baking sheet, make 4 evenly spaced mounds of cheese, 2 table-spoons each. Tap the side of the pan gently so that cheese spreads out into circles roughly 3 inches in diameter. Bake for exactly 5 minutes. Let cool for 15 seconds, then pick up each individual cheese circle by its edge with a metal spatula and drape it over an upturned shot glass. Move quickly. After all 4 Parmesan cups are in place, use your fingers to gently mold them around the glasses. Let cool for 2 minutes, then lift Parmesan cups off the glasses. Repeat the whole process until you have 12 cups. Reserve.

To a blender or small food processor, add oil, garlic, lemon juice, Dijon, vinegar, anchovies, Worcestershire, salt, and pepper. Purée. Add egg yolk and pulse a couple of times. Reserve.

Just before assembling, toss lettuce with 2 tablespoons dressing. Add more dressing if desired.

To assemble, line up Parmesan cups, fill with salad, and top each with a crouton.

uncommon goods 4 shot glasses; nonstick baking sheet

level of difficulty Making the Parmesan cups requires the same quali-ties as a good lover: An unrushed manner and an easy touch.

active prep 45 minutes

cooking time 15 minutes

shortcuts Use a store-bought Caesar dressing.

advance work Parmesan cups and Caesar dressing can be made earlier in the day. Always wait until the last moment to toss the salad.

music to cook by Cat Stevens, *Teaser & the Firecat* will almost make you wish he hadn't found Allah, changed his name, and retired from the music biz.

liquid assets A Chablis or other crisp, non-oaked Chardonnay is lean and mean enough for the richness of the dressing and the dominance of the cheese.

cauliflower popcorn

Who woulda thunk that cauliflower could actually become addictive? With this simple high-temperature roasting process known as caramelization, your basic off-the-rack cauliflower is miraculously transformed into sweet, lip-smackin' candy bombs your guests won't be able to get enough of. You'll find yourself having newfound respect for a vegetable you deleted from your Palm Pilot years ago.

1 head cauliflower

4 tablespoons olive oil

1 tablespoon salt (or, for a salt-free alternative, Mrs. Dash Table blend)

Preheat oven to 425°F.

Cut out and discard cauliflower core and thick stems. Trim remaining cauliflower into florets the size of golf balls. In a large bowl, add cauliflower, olive oil, and salt. Toss thoroughly.

Spread cauliflower on a baking sheet (lined with parchment paper, if available, for easy cleanup). Roast for 1 hour, or until much of each floret has become golden brown. (That's the caramelization process converting the dormant natural sugars into sweetness. The browner the florets, the sweeter they will taste.) Turn 3 or 4 times during roasting.

Use crumpled up aluminum foil or paper towels to create a false bottom in your popcorn container, fill it with cauliflower, and serve immediately.

uncommon goods an empty movie theater popcorn container or aluminum Jiffy Pop package

level of difficulty The same as making real popcorn.

active prep 10 minutes

cooking time 1 hour

shortcuts Buy the precut cauliflower in the lazy boy section of the produce department.

advance work Raw cauliflower can be precut and refrigerated for up to 2 days in an airtight bag or a bowl of water. With minimal sacrifice, cauliflower can be cooked earlier in the day and reheated in a 450°F oven for 10 minutes.

music to cook by James Brown, *The Popcorn* has Soul Brother #1 servin' up some tasty treats.

liquid assets Big buttery Chardonnays may have fallen out of fashion, but they are the perfect pairing for this equally uncelebrated cruciferous vegetable.

byzantine bruschetta

Heirloom tomatoes are grown from seeds of ancient tomato strains. Unlike their commercial cousins that are cross-pollinated to improve their shipability, shelf life, and usefulness in a game of catch, these tomatoes actually smell and taste like . . . tomatoes. And if that's not enough, they come in curious shapes and a kaleidoscope of colors—making each bite an edible work of art.

1 sourdough or country-style bâtarde (a 3-inch-diameter baguette)**, sliced**

4 cloves garlic

1/3 cup best-available extra-virgin olive oil

Freshly ground black pepper

6 fresh basil leaves, chopped or finely sliced

8 heirloom tomatoes of assorted colors and sizes, thinly sliced

Salt (ideally one of those fancy sea salts you splurged for)

Toast 12 slices of bread in a toaster or oven until they are very brown.

Immediately after removing the bread from the toaster, rub a garlic clove over the entire surface of one side. Each slice should use up about 1/4 to 1/3 of a clove. (Be careful; when the garlic meets the toast's hot surface, it will create fumes that sting your eyes—just like an onion.)

To assemble, generously drizzle olive oil over each slice. Sprinkle with a generous amount of pepper and basil. Top with 3 different-colored, different-sized tomato slices. Sprinkle with salt.

uncommon goods heirloom tomatoes (available at farmers' markets), which may be replaced with conventionally grown red and yellow tomatoes

level of difficulty Really, really easy.

active prep 20 minutes

shortcuts Dice the tomatoes, garlic, and basil, and mix them in a bowl with olive oil, salt, and pepper. At showtime, simply toast bread and spoon the tomato mixture overtop.

advance work The bread can be sliced and the garlic peeled earlier in the day; the tomatoes should be sliced no more than 1/2 hour before serving; toasting and assembling should be done just before serving.

music to cook by Nick Cave and the Bad Seeds, *No More Shall We Part* is a haunting treasure trove of musical novellas.

liquid assets A Pinot Grigio has the high level of acidity necessary to do the dance with the natural acidity of the tomatoes.

french fried polenta

yield: 18 bites

Contrary to what their name suggests, French fries are a Belgian creation. Here's what I imagine would have happened if the Italians had gotten into the act.

1½ **cups polenta** (the 5-minute version or the traditional variety)

3 **cups chicken or vegetable stock**

½ **cup freshly grated Parmigiano-Reggiano cheese**

1 **tablespoon stemmed fresh thyme, minced, or 1 teaspoon dried thyme**

1 **tablespoon white truffle oil** (optional)

2 **tablespoons olive oil**

Salt

Cook polenta according to directions, but replace water with stock. Just before finishing, stir in Parmigiano-Reggiano, thyme, and truffle oil.

In a 9-x-13-inch baking dish, add 1 tablespoon water. Transfer polenta to baking dish and spread evenly until it is ½ inch in thickness. Smooth surface with a spatula. Refrigerate for 1 hour, or until it solidifies.

Turn baking dish upside down and remove polenta in 1 slab. Slice into strips the size and shape of chunky fries.

In a large nonstick pan over medium-high heat, add olive oil and polenta fries. Do your best to keep the polenta fries from touching. Pan fry for approximately 3 minutes per side, or until a golden brown crispy crust has formed on each of the 4 sides. Season with salt.

uncommon goods truffle oil (available at gourmet food stores for about $10 for a 2-ounce bottle); a fast-food French fry container

the adventure club Replace truffle oil with a shaved truffle.

level of difficulty About the same as making real French fries.

active prep 45 minutes

inactive prep 1 hour

cooking time 15 minutes

shortcuts Take everyone to McDonald's.

advance work Polenta can be cooked and sliced up to 2 days in advance. With minimal sacrifice, it can also be pan fried earlier in the day and reheated in a 450°F oven for 10 minutes.

music to cook by Jeff Buckley, *Grace* is the melancholy, brooding debut from a sadly missed artist that has kept me company through many lonely hours in the kitchen.

liquid assets The easy-drinking Italian Barbera is perfect for offsetting the richness of the truffled polenta.

rings of fire

I love crispy onion rings and I love intense hot sauces. So for me, bringing them together is an exercise in efficiency. The result is a winning combination that is deceptively easy to make. Capsaicin junkies should replace the Tabasco with any sauce that has "insanity," "inferno," or "sphincter" in its title.

2 Vidalia onions or other sweet onion

1½ cups flour

2 serrano chiles, minced (plus a couple in reserve)

2 teaspoons salt + more to season finished rings

1 teaspoon cayenne pepper

½ teaspoon freshly ground black pepper

1 cup beer

1 tablespoon Tabasco (ideally chipotle Tabasco)

3 cups peanut oil for frying

Slice onions in ¼-inch slices and separate into rings. Select the 12 largest, most aesthetically pleasing rings.

In a medium bowl, add 1 cup of the flour, the serranos, 2 teaspoons salt, cayenne, and pepper. Slowly whisk in beer and add hot sauce. The batter should be the consistency of thin pancake batter.

In a medium, tall pot, heat oil to 350°F (see Fear of Frying, page 126).

In a medium bowl, add remaining ½ cup flour. Toss onion rings in flour to coat. Shake off excess flour.

Dip one onion ring in batter until thoroughly coated, then fry for approximately 2 minutes, or until golden. Turn once during frying. Remove and drain on paper towels. Let cool, then season with salt, and taste. Count to 30, then assess the heat level. Add more of everything hot according to your pain threshold (and that of your guests). Continue frying rings in small batches and serve immediately.

level of difficulty The hardest part is figuring out what to do with the other 5 beers.

active prep 20 minutes

cooking time 10 minutes

shortcuts Skip the serranos and the Tabasco and just add more cayenne. Or skip the serranos and the cayenne and just add more Tabasco, or . . .

advance work Batter can be prepared and onions can be sliced earlier in the day.

multiplicity Existing batter will accommodate another batch of onions.

music to cook by Johnny Cash, *Ring of Fire/The Best of Johnny Cash*. The taste of love may be sweet, but onion rings will never break your heart and run off with your best friend.

liquid assets See "level of difficulty."

bee stings

No pigs, cows, or bees were harmed in the making of this tiny taste explosion. But it would not be possible without the precious yield of their respective foraging, milk producing, and honey making. Thanks to their hard work, this is the least amount of effort you will ever have to expend for the greatest number of accolades.

1/4 **cup best-available honey**

1/2 **tablespoon white truffle oil**

1/4 **teaspoon freshly ground black pepper**

6-ounce block Parmigiano-Reggiano cheese

In a small bowl, combine honey, truffle oil, and pepper. Reserve.

Just before serving, use a paring knife to chisel cheese into irregular 1/2-inch nuggets. Drizzle truffled honey over each nugget.

To get the most Parmigiano-Reggiano for your buck, look for rindless center cuts, and avoid pieces that have disproportionate amounts of rind. For the freshest Parmigiano-Reggiano, purchase from stores that seem to move a lot of it.

uncommon goods truffle oil (available at gourmet food stores for about $10 for a 2-ounce bottle)

level of difficulty n/a

active prep 5 minutes

shortcuts Skip the truffled honey and drizzle cheese with an aged balsamic vinegar. Or just serve the cheese au naturel.

advance work Truffled honey can be mixed and Parmigiano can be cut up to 2 days in advance. Wrap cheese tightly in plastic wrap to keep it from drying out.

multiplicity You can double the cheese without the need for more truffled honey.

music to cook by PJ Harvey, *To Bring You My Love* is a scorching disc from an alternative darling who really is the bee's knees.

liquid assets If you are lucky enough to have—or know someone who has—an old bottle of champagne, you're in for a treat. The toasty, yeasty characteristics of vintage bubbly are an elegant and sophisticated foil for the earthiness of the truffle oil. The rest of us can enjoy an Australian Sémillon blend with honey undertones that will play off the nutty sweetness of the cheese and the drizzle.

gazpacholé

Gazpacho is a Spanish classic. The twist here is in the presentation. Sipping it from a frozen tomato cup adds to the pleasure of this refreshing summer soup. Finally, a use for all those tomatoes that seem to ripen at exactly the same time.

16 aesthetically pleasing, medium, firm tomatoes (4 are back-ups)

2 medium celery stalks, chopped

3/4 cup canned tomato juice

1/2 cucumber, peeled, seeds discarded

1/2 red bell pepper, seeds discarded, chopped

1/3 cup stemmed, lightly packed fresh cilantro

2 green onions, chopped

1 1/2 jalapeño peppers, seeds discarded, minced

3 tablespoons olive oil

2 tablespoons freshly squeezed lemon juice

1 clove garlic, minced

1 tablespoon balsamic or red wine vinegar

Salt

Freshly ground black pepper

12 goldfish crackers for garnish

level of difficulty Scooping out the tomatoes requires a modest amount of dexterity and sobriety. Making the gazpacho is just like blending a smoothie, but with a few more ingredients.

active prep 45 minutes

inactive prep 2 hours

shortcuts Serve gazpacho in shot glasses or mini paper cups.

advance work Tomato cups can be prepared and frozen several days in advance; gazpacho can be made (and even gets better) up to 2 days in advance.

music to cook by Jane's Addiction, *Ritual de lo Habitual* is the signature sound of the Lollapalooza era.

liquid assets Cava is a Spanish sparkling wine that will be right at home at this tomatofest.

Slice 1/2 inch off the top end of each tomato. Hollow out the tomato with a grapefruit spoon, regular spoon, or melon baller. Reserve the tomato flesh. Select the 12 most aesthetically pleasing tomato cups, place them on a wax paper–lined plate in the freezer for 1 hour, or until frozen solid.

Transfer 2 1/2 cups of tomato flesh and all of the remaining ingredients (except salt, pepper, and goldfish) to a blender or food processor. Purée. Chill in refrigerator for a minimum of 2 hours. Season with salt and pepper. Serve in frozen tomato cups. Garnish with a goldfish.

cucumber shooters

yield: 12 shooters

Here's an opportunity to transform the humble field cucumber into a mixed-media art project. All it takes are a couple of common kitchen utensils to turn the ends of the cukes into sculpted vessels, and a few basic ingredients to turn what's left into a zippy and refreshing green gazpacho.

8 cucumbers (the conventional field variety)

1/4 cup stemmed fresh mint

1 shallot, minced

1 jalapeño pepper, seeds discarded, minced

2 tablespoons freshly squeezed lime juice

1 clove garlic, minced

4 tablespoons extra-virgin olive oil

2 tablespoons champagne vinegar or white wine vinegar

Salt

Freshly ground black pepper

Cut 2 1/2 inches off both ends of the cucumbers. Reserve.

Peel middle sections, cut in half lengthwise, and use a spoon to scrape out seeds. Discard seeds.

continued

In a food processor, add the middle sections of the cucumbers along with the mint, shallot, jalapeño, lime juice, and garlic. Purée.

Strain puréed mixture through a fine strainer into a medium bowl. Use a rubber spatula to press out as much juice as possible from the mash. Discard solids. Whisk in oil and vinegar, and season with salt and pepper. Refrigerate for a minimum of 1 hour.

Take the 12 most aesthetically pleasing cucumber ends and slice off the bottom $1/4$ inch so that they stand solidly on their ends. Use a zester, paring knife, or vegetable peeler to create designs in the peel. Use a melon baller or a tiny spoon to scoop out the seeds and some of the surrounding cucumber, creating cucumber shot glasses. Serve the chilled cucumber gazpacho in the sculpted cups.

uncommon goods food processor; zester (the kind with a V-shaped groove in it to make lemon twists)

level of difficulty Just like arts and crafts in school; everyone can do it, some will just make it look prettier.

active prep 1 hour

inactive prep 1 hour

shortcuts Serve gazpacho in shot glasses or mini paper cups.

advance work Gazpacho can be made up to 2 days in advance; cucumber cups can be sculpted earlier in the day and refrigerated in plastic wrap.

music to cook by Patti Smith, *Horses* is an album I originally owned on 8-track, and it is as cool (as a cucumber) today as it was then.

lovin' spoonfuls

yield: 12 bites

These crispy comforting polenta bites nestled in a creamy red bell pepper sauce are perfect for Valentine's Day, romantic dinners, and anytime you just want to eat your heart out.

roasted red bell pepper sauce

1 tablespoon olive oil

1 shallot, diced

2 roasted red bell peppers (canned or jarred are just fine)

½ cup chicken or vegetable stock

½ jalapeño pepper, seeds discarded

1 tablespoon stemmed fresh thyme

1 tablespoon freshly squeezed lemon juice

3 tablespoons heavy cream

Salt

Freshly ground black pepper

polenta

¾ cup polenta (the 5-minute version or the traditional variety)

1½ cups chicken or vegetable stock

¼ cup freshly grated Parmigiano-Reggiano cheese

2 tablespoons olive oil

continued

In a sauté pan over medium heat, heat the oil and add the shallot. Cook for about 4 minutes, stirring frequently, or until the shallot just begins to show signs of browning.

Add the bell peppers, stock, jalapeño, and thyme. Bring to a boil, then immediately lower heat and simmer for 15 minutes. Remove from heat and let cool.

In a food processor or blender, add pan contents and lemon juice. Blend until smooth. Reserve.

Cook polenta according to directions, but replace water with stock. Just before finishing, stir in Parmigiano-Reggiano.

In a 9-x-13-inch baking dish, add 1 tablespoon water. Transfer polenta to baking dish and spread evenly until it is $1/4$ inch in thickness. Refrigerate for 1 hour, or until it solidifies.

Use a 1-inch heart-shaped cookie cutter or a paring knife to cut out hearts.

In a sauté pan over medium-high heat, add oil and sauté polenta hearts for approximately 3 minutes per side, or until a golden brown crispy crust has formed on each side. Transfer to paper towels to drain.

Before serving, reheat sauce in a saucepan and stir in cream. Season to taste with salt and pepper.

To assemble, roll up a cloth napkin and set it down on a serving platter. Rest spoon handles on napkin so that the spoon cups are level. Fill each spoon halfway with red pepper sauce and top with a polenta heart.

uncommon goods 1-inch heart-shaped cookie cutter; large soup spoons

level of difficulty Like a long straight staircase, there are many steps, but if you take them one at a time, there is nothing to trip you up.

active prep 35 minutes

inactive prep 1 hour

cooking time 35–60 minutes

shortcuts Use a store-bought red bell pepper sauce or pasta sauce.

advance work Red bell pepper sauce can be made up to 2 days in advance. Polenta can be cooked and die-cut up to 2 days in advance. With minimal sacrifice, it can also be pan fried earlier in the day and reheated in a 450°F oven for 5 minutes.

music to cook by The Lovin' Spoonful, *Do You Believe in Magic* is a free-wheeling classic from the summer of '65.

liquid assets A simple Primitivo, the Italian cousin of Zinfandel, is a hearty complement to this dressed-up peasant dish.

sweets

egg creams, page 98

egg creams

This high-concept white chocolate mousse and mango dessert is my homage to Ferrán Adriá, the culinary envelope-pusher behind Spain's celebrated El Bulli restaurant. It looks like a soft-boiled egg, and runs like a soft-boiled egg, but one spoonful will reveal that the tasty yolk is on your guests.

2 ripe mangos, peeled and pitted

12 eggs

3/4 teaspoon unflavored gelatin

8 ounces white baker's chocolate, chopped into teeny-weeny bits

1 1/2 cups cold heavy cream

1 teaspoon vanilla extract

Place mangos in a blender and purée. Pour into one or more plastic containers so the purée is 3/4 of an inch deep. Cover and freeze for 2 hours, or until frozen solid.

Using a sharp knife, carefully chop the tops off the eggs as you would a soft-boiled egg. Reserve the eggs for breakfast and run the egg shells under scalding hot water (be careful) to clean out any egg white residue. Reserve shells in egg carton for safekeeping.

In a small bowl, add 3 tablespoons water. Sprinkle gelatin overtop and let stand for 5 minutes.

In a medium heatproof bowl, add chocolate.

In a small pot, bring 1/2 cup of the cream to a boil. Add dissolved gelatin and vanilla and stir for 30 seconds. Pour cream over chocolate and whisk until smooth. Refrigerate for 30 minutes, or until chocolate thickens but still falls off a spoon.

In a stand mixer or large bowl, whip remaining 1 cup cream until it forms stiff peaks. Using a rubber spatula, gently but thoroughly fold whipped cream into chocolate mixture. Return to refrigerator for 2 hours, or until it has set.

Remove frozen mango from containers, and slice into ¾-inch cubes. Using a paring knife, sculpt mango cubes into yolk-shaped balls. Reserve mango yolks in freezer.

 To assemble, transfer chocolate mousse (that's what it is now) to a pastry bag or a large resealable plastic bag with its corner clipped (see diagram). Fill one-third of each egg shell with mousse. Set 1 mango yolk in the center of each shell and push it down slightly into mousse. Pipe more mousse over yolk, being careful not to leave any air pockets, and fill shell to just below the top. Return to the refrigerator for a minimum of 1 hour to allow the mango yolks to thaw (so that they run when cut into).

uncommon goods gelatin; white baker's chocolate

the adventure club Cut the eggs at the bottom instead of the top. After filling the eggs with mousse, seal with a plug of melted white chocolate. After the chocolate hardens, serve the eggs in egg cups, plug-sides down, thereby creating the illusion that the eggs have not been tampered with.

level of difficulty Like an elaborate card trick. Seems tricky to pull off at the outset, but when decoded is actually quite simple.

active prep 1 hour

inactive prep 4 hours

shortcuts Go high-concept or go home.

advance work Eggs can be made up to 2 days in advance. Refrigerate in an egg carton wrapped with plastic wrap.

music to cook by ABBA, *Gold: Greatest Hits* is full of classics I hated in the disco days but can't resist now.

liquid assets Moscato d'Asti is a semi-sweet Italian sparkling wine that is just light and fruity enough to support the overt sweetness of the white chocolate mousse.

pearls of wisdom

Who gives a damn about finding a pearl when you get a creamy hazelnut-infused white chocolate truffle inside these oyster shells—each time, every time?

○·○

8 ounces white chocolate, cut into tiny bits

3 ounces cream cheese, at room temperature

1/2 cup powdered sugar

1 tablespoon Frangelico (or amaretto, Grand Marnier, Cointreau . . .)

1/4 teaspoon vanilla extract

Oyster shells (optional)

Colored sugar for presentation (optional)

In a medium pot, add 2 inches of water and bring to a boil. Reduce to a simmer and place a medium glass or metal bowl over the pot. Add half the chocolate and stir until it is fully melted. Turn off heat. Let cool slightly.

In a medium bowl, beat cream cheese and powdered sugar until smooth. Slowly stir melted chocolate into cream cheese mixture. Add Frangelico and vanilla and stir until mixture is smooth. Let cool, then spread out 3/4 inch thick on a wax paper–covered baking sheet. Freeze for 2 hours, or until hard (it won't actually freeze).

Set out a rack over a baking sheet. No rack? Take the rack out of the toaster oven.

Cut truffle mixture into 3/4-inch squares and roll each square between the palms of your hands until it becomes a perfect ball about the diameter of a quarter. Reserve in the refrigerator.

Melt remaining chocolate over a water bath like before. Transfer chocolate to a small bowl.

Toss truffles, one at a time, into chocolate. Roll with a fork until fully coated. Remove and set on the rack. Refrigerate for another hour. If desired, serve in oyster shells lined with colored sugar.

uncommon goods oyster shell bottom halves, scrubbed with an abrasive pad, and run through a dishwasher (beg them from an oyster bar)

level of difficulty If you can double-boil water, you can make this.

active prep 1 hour

inactive prep 3 hours

shortcuts Skip the final chocolate coating step and finish the truffles by dusting them with powdered sugar.

advance work Truffles can be made a week in advance and refrigerated.

music to cook by Janis Joplin, *Pearl* is the soulful album that was sadly her last.

liquid assets A sparkling Muscat, light and low in alcohol, will add some sparkle to the richness of the truffle.

nutcases

This savory little dessert is like a one-bite cheese course. The pungent, slightly salty flavor of the Gorgonzola, the sweetness of the honey, and the spiciness of the nuts will drive your taste buds crazy.

20 walnuts in the shell (These are being used for their shells only, since the nuts usually turn into shrapnel when they are opened by hand.)

1 teaspoon sugar

1/4 teaspoon salt

1/8 teaspoon cayenne pepper

24 cosmetically perfect walnut halves (Be sure to select packages that say walnut "halves" not just "pieces.")

1 tablespoon canola oil

1 cup demerara sugar (for presentation)

6 ounces Gorgonzola cheese, at room temperature

3 tablespoons honey

Preheat oven to 350°F.

Insert a paring knife into the small opening at the top of each walnut shell and twist it to split the shell in half. (Don't hate me when some break into several pieces in all the wrong places. This is an inexact science and some walnuts are much more difficult to split evenly than others—hence the spare shells.) Clean out the nut and casings and eat the little walnut fragments. Reserve the empty shells.

In a small bowl, combine sugar, salt, and cayenne. In a medium bowl, toss walnut halves with oil. Sprinkle nuts with sugar mixture and toss thoroughly. Transfer nuts to a baking sheet and roast for 10 minutes, or until browned and toasted. Let cool to room temperature.

To assemble, spread demerara sugar on a plate and set walnut shells in sugar. Sandwich 1 teaspoon of cheese between 2 walnut halves. Then place mini walnut sandwich upright in a walnut shell. Just before serving, drizzle honey over each mini walnut sandwich (or walnut brain—depending on your mindset).

uncommon goods whole walnuts in their shells

level of difficulty Like breaking into your own house; once you successfully crack the nut, there is nothing else to worry about.

active prep 25 minutes

cooking time 10 minutes

shortcuts Use store-bought spiced nuts and/or skip the whole shell deal and serve the cheese-stuffed nuts on their backs.

advance work Whole nuts can be split anytime, and the walnut halves can be seasoned and roasted up to 2 days in advance; the assembly can be done hours in advance, except for the honey, which should be drizzled at the last second.

music to cook by The Jesus and Mary Chain, *Psychocandy* is just like honey—but with more feedback.

liquid assets A Sauternes, late harvest wine, ice wine, or a port will all work magically in their own individual ways.

lemongrass licks

These popsicles exemplify my approach to creating recipes: Start with anything you loved as a kid, make the flavors a little more sophisticated, add a little booze—and presto, an adult sensation is born.

layer #1

1½ mangos, peeled and pitted

2 tablespoons freshly squeezed lime juice

2 tablespoons Cointreau

1 tablespoon peeled and grated fresh ginger

layer #2

1 cup whole strawberries, hulled

1 peach, peeled and pitted

1 tablespoon sugar

layer #3

1½ ripe bananas

6 tablespoons guava juice

3 tablespoons dark rum

12 stalks lemongrass, outer layers trimmed and cut 4 inches long from the bottom end

uncommon goods pony glasses, shot glasses, Tupperware-style popsicle molds, or mini Dixie cups; lemongrass stalks

level of difficulty Kids make this stuff all the time.

active prep 30 minutes

inactive prep 3 hours

shortcuts To cut the freezing time by two-thirds, limit each pop to 1 flavor.

advance work Can be made eons in advance. Seal the exposed end with plastic wrap to prevent freezer burn.

music to cook by Brad Mehldau, *Songs: The Art of The Trio, Vol. 3* is the place to start if you're not familiar with this contemporary jazz pianist.

In a blender, purée the ingredients for each individual layer and reserve the mixtures in separate containers.

Set out 12 mini popsicle molds or suitable alternatives and fill each of them one-third full with mango mixture. Place a small square of aluminum foil over each mold and crimp it snugly around the top of the mold. Use the tip of a paring knife to cut a ¼-inch slit in the middle of each piece of foil. Slide a lemongrass skewer, thin-side down, through the slit to the bottom of each mold.

Freeze molds for approximately 1 hour, or until frozen. Fill each mold another third of the way with strawberry mixture. Return to freezer until frozen. Top molds with banana mixture and return to freezer until frozen.

To remove pops, dip molds into hot water for a few seconds, then twist pops out.

s'more shooters

This rich chocolatey indulgence is a grown-up version of the campfire classic.

12 large marshmallows

1 cup half & half

8 ounces best-available-quality bittersweet chocolate, chopped into teeny-weeny bits

1½ cups milk

¾ cup amaretto

½ cup graham cracker crumbs

Toast marshmallows over a campfire or stovetop until golden brown. Let cool and reserve.

In a small pot, bring half & half to a boil. In a medium bowl, add chocolate. Pour cream over chocolate and stir until chocolate has fully melted.

Return chocolate ganache to the pot and whisk in milk. Over medium heat, bring to a simmer and stir in ½ cup amaretto.

Pour remaining amaretto into a small bowl so that it is ¼ inch deep and place graham cracker crumbs on a small saucer ¼ inch deep. To assemble, dip the rims of the shot glasses in amaretto, then in the graham cracker crumbs. Fill glasses with hot chocolate and top each with a toasted marshmallow (make your life easier by transferring the hot chocolate first to a measuring cup with a spout).

uncommon goods shot glasses

level of difficulty Any camper can make these.

active prep 10 minutes

cooking time 20 minutes

shortcuts Don't bother toasting the marshmallows.

advance work Hot chocolate can be made up to 2 days in advance. Marshmallows can be toasted, and glasses rimmed, earlier in the day.

music to cook by Hot Chocolate, *Hot Chocolate* is a sexy dance party.

coffee crisp

Making creamy, sweet, custardy crème brûlée is a no-brainer—except for the tricky bit at the very end where you have to make like a welder and caramelize the sugar with a blowtorch. Fortunately, using your broiler instead can minimize the challenge.

6 egg yolks

8 tablespoons sugar

2 tablespoons instant espresso or coffee powder (the freeze-dried stuff)

1½ cups heavy cream

½ teaspoon vanilla extract

Preheat oven to 300°F.

In a medium bowl, whisk egg yolks and 6 tablespoons of the sugar for 1 minute, or until smooth and pale yellow in color. Reserve.

In a second medium bowl, add espresso granules and ¼ cup of the cream. Whisk until smooth, then add remaining cream and vanilla, and whisk until well blended.

Very gently, fold espresso cream mixture into egg yolks.

Use a ladle to pour custard mixture into espresso cups, filling them three-fourths of the way to the top.

Place cups in a baking dish or roasting pan and transfer to oven. Fill a pitcher with warm tap water. Before closing oven door, pour water into pan (but not into the cups themselves!) until it reaches halfway up the sides of the cups.

Bake for 40 minutes, or until the custards jiggle just slightly when you shake the pan. Remove pan from oven and leave out on counter, allowing the residual heat of the water to finish the cooking process.

When custards have fully solidified, refrigerate for 2 hours.

Just before serving, sprinkle ½ teaspoon of sugar evenly overtop each custard. Use a small blowtorch to caramelize the sugar. Alternatively, place cups 1 inch below oven broiler under a watchful eye for approximately 2 minutes, or until sugar caramelizes.

uncommon goods espresso cups, blowtorch

level of difficulty True, you have to make like a welder, but you don't have to do it while balancing on a steel beam.

active prep 25 minutes

inactive prep 2 hours

cooking time 40 minutes

shortcuts Skip dessert.

advance work Custards can be made up to 2 days in advance. Caramelizing the sugar must be done at the last minute.

music to cook by Peggy Lee, *Black Coffee* is absolute torch, no twang.

liquid assets Hard-core caffeine junkies should serve with a demitasse of real espresso.

dog bones

yield: 24 biscuits

Generous amounts of freshly grated ginger and white pepper give these gingerbread cookies real bite.

2 cups sugar

1 cup salted butter, at room temperature

2/3 cup molasses

2 eggs

3 tablespoons peeled and finely grated fresh ginger

1/2 tablespoon apple cider vinegar (needed to react with the baking soda)

6 cups all-purpose flour + extra to dust rolling surface

2 tablespoons white pepper

1 tablespoon ground cinnamon

1 1/2 teaspoons baking soda

1/2 teaspoon ground cloves

Preheat oven to 325°F.

In a large bowl, combine sugar, butter, molasses, eggs, ginger, and vinegar.

In a second large bowl, combine 6 cups flour, pepper, cinnamon, baking soda, and cloves.

Blend the contents of bowl #2 into bowl #1.

Wrap dough in plastic wrap and refrigerate for 1 hour (this allows the dough to harden so that it can be rolled out).

Sprinkle rolling surface with flour. Roll out dough to 3/8 inch in thickness.

Use a 3-inch bone-shaped cookie cutter to stamp out cookies. After cutting the first batch, knead the trimmings together and reroll. Bake on a baking sheet for 12–15 minutes, or until they begin to brown.

uncommon goods empty dog biscuit box; dog bone–shaped cookie cutter

level of difficulty As easy as baking cookies.

active prep 30 minutes

inactive prep 1 hour

cooking time 15 minutes

shortcuts Skip the doggie theme.

advance work Dough or fully baked cookies can be made days in advance.

music to cook by George Thorogood & the Destroyers, *Bad to the Bone* is B-B-bluesy slide guitar rock.

liquid assets Baileys Irish Cream on the rocks is the milk that will mellow the spiciness of these cookies.

carrot cake shooters

yield: 12 shooters

During a recent culinary retrofitting, I spent a week working as a prep cook in the kitchen at Campanile—one of the most acclaimed restaurants in Los Angeles and a pioneer of California cuisine. One day, I observed the pastry chef roasting and juicing carrots for her carrot ice cream (that's California cuisine for you). The resulting juice, to which she added a small splash of vanilla, instantly reminded me of carrot cake. It's moments like this I live for. Racing back to my own kitchen, I re-created the juice and added a few other spices and ingredients commonly used in carrot cake. Over time I discovered that reducing store-bought carrot juice achieves close enough results with a fraction of the fuss. The concept of drinking liquid carrot cake may seem hard to grasp at first, but one sip will make you a believer.

1 quart store-bought or homemade fresh carrot juice

½ cup heavy cream

¼ cup sugar

3 tablespoons pineapple juice

2 tablespoons walnut oil (optional)

2 teaspoons vanilla extract

½ teaspoon ground cinnamon

½ teaspoon ground nutmeg

¼ teaspoon ground allspice

¼ teaspoon ground cloves

12 carrot tops, sliced off ½ inch below the greens (for presentation)

In a medium pot over medium-high heat, reduce the carrot juice by half. This should take about 20 minutes.

Whisk in all remaining ingredients (except the carrot tops).

Serve in pony glasses and garnish with carrot tops.

uncommon goods carrot juice; pony glasses

the adventure club Make roasted carrot juice: Start with 5 pounds of carrots, brush with butter, and roast in a 400°F oven for 30 minutes, then juice.

level of difficulty About the same as talking on the phone while choosing a pair of shoes to match your outfit.

active prep 10 minutes

cooking time 20 minutes

shortcuts Let your fingers do the walking to find out who carries fresh carrot juice.

advance work The carrot juice can be reduced and seasoned up to 2 days in advance. Reheat just before serving.

music to cook by Warner Bros. Symphony Orchestra, *Bugs Bunny on Broadway* is a mix of classic Bugs Bunny scores for anyone who's a fan of cartoon music.

hangover helpers

yield: 12 bites

Blame it on my twisted, surreal sense of humor, but nothing seems funnier than seeing your friends drinking (what looks like) Pepto-Bismol, with a straw. But read on, the prank is not without its sweet rewards.

3 cups fresh strawberries, hulled, or frozen strawberries, thawed

3 cups vanilla ice cream

1½ cups milk

¾ cup Chambord or framboise (raspberry liqueurs)

In a blender, purée ingredients in two batches. Serve in Pepto-Bismol bottles or similar facsimiles, with straws.

uncommon goods 4-ounce Pepto-Bismol bottles, emptied and cleaned

level of difficulty As easy as making a milkshake—which, not coincidentally, is what you are doing.

active prep 5 minutes

shortcuts Use strawberry ice cream.

advance work Strawberries can be hulled up to a day in advance.

music to cook by AC/DC, *Back in Black*. For those about to rock, I salute you.

honey do shooters

During that brief window of opportunity each year when melons are as fragrant as French perfume, a minute in the food processor is virtually all it takes to transform their sweet green flesh into the nectar of the gods.

1 cantaloupe melon, halved, seeds discarded

1 ripe honeydew melon, halved, seeds discarded

1/4 cup stemmed fresh mint leaves

3 tablespoons freshly squeezed lime juice

1/4 cup ice wine or Sauternes (optional)

Use a large melon baller or small ice-cream scoop to scoop out twelve 1-inch cantaloupe balls. Reserve.

Scoop out honeydew flesh. Transfer to a blender along with mint and lime juice. Purée.

Strain purée through a fine strainer and discard solids. Stir in ice wine, if desired. Chill for a minimum of 1 hour.

Serve in pony glasses and top each with a cantaloupe ball.

uncommon goods pony glasses; melon baller

level of difficulty The only challenge is selecting a ripe melon (use the smell test).

active prep 30 minutes

inactive prep 1 hour

shortcuts Skip the cantaloupe and garnish with mint leaves.

advance work Honeydew purée can be made up to a day in advance.

music to cook by The Honeydrippers, *Sea of Love* marks Robert Plant's return to his pre-Zeppelin roots.

ice breakers

Ice wine is made in cold-climate countries from grapes that are allowed to hang on the vines well into the winter months. The sugar-laden grapes are hand-picked and immediately pressed in their frozen state, yielding just a few precious droplets of intensely flavored grape must. Now you know why ice wine is so heavenly . . . and so expensive. And why, when you drizzle a bit of it over crushed frozen juice, you create a snow cone that could make angels sing.

1 quart store-bought or homemade peach, blackberry, or raspberry juice

1 cup ice wine

Pour juice into 2 ice trays and freeze for 3 hours, or until frozen solid.

Pop frozen fruit juice cubes out of trays. Crush cubes in an ice crusher or blender.

Use a small ice-cream scoop to spoon crushed ice into mini snow cone cups or paper cups. Drizzle with ice wine.

uncommon goods mini paper cups or snow cone cups (see uncommon goods, page 66)

level of difficulty Insanely easy.

active prep 10 minutes

inactive prep 3 hours

shortcuts Serve ice wine over plain crushed ice . . . or just serve ice wine.

advance work Juice can be frozen and crushed eons in advance, then returned to the freezer.

music to cook by Fats Waller, *Breakin' the Ice: The Early Years, Part 1* is a collection of the original recordings from 1934–35 that made the brilliant stride pianist famous.

knuckle sandwich

Full disclosure: I am a closet wrestling fan. So you can imagine how starstruck I was when two world champion wrestlers from the WWE—Trish Stratus and Val Venus—joined me in my Toastermobile for an episode of my TV show. After a dinner of mussels and bricked chicken, they tossed me around a ring, kicked me in the stomach, and stomped on my head—it was sooo much fun. I invented this dessert in their honor. The whole hazelnuts are bone-crunchingly loud when you bite into the sandwich. It won't hurt, but it is messy.

3/4 cup whole hazelnuts, ideally blanched (skinned)

2 tablespoons butter

2 pears, skin on, cut into 1/8-inch-thick slices, then cored

1 store-bought pound cake

6 tablespoons Nutella or other chocolate-hazelnut spread

Preheat oven to 350°F.

Put hazelnuts on a baking sheet and bake for 12 minutes, or until they begin to brown. If hazelnuts are still in their skins, bake until skins begin to darken, or for blanched nuts, until they turn golden. Remove from oven and let cool. If hazelnuts are still in their skins, place nuts in the center of a clean dishtowel, fold the towel around the nuts, and rub vigorously between both hands for 15 seconds to release the skins. Discard skins and reserve the nuts.

In a sauté pan over medium heat (err on the low side of medium), melt butter and sauté pear slices for approximately 5 minutes per side, or until they begin to brown. Reserve.

Cut 6 slices of pound cake, 1/4 inch thick. Toast pound cake in a toaster oven, or on a baking sheet in a 300°F oven. (It will fall apart in an upright toaster.)

Smear 3 cake slices with Nutella. Cover entire Nutella surface with hazelnuts, then press them into the Nutella. Top with a layer of pear slices and cover with second slice of pound cake. Secure each knuckle sandwich with 4 toothpicks, then cut into 4 pieces.

uncommon goods toothpicks with curly tops

level of difficulty The wrestlers mastered it on their first attempt.

active prep 40 minutes

shortcuts Buy skinned hazelnuts, and don't bother roasting them.

advance work Nuts can be roasted several days in advance.

music to cook by Various Artists, *World Wrestling Federation: The Anthology* brings together all the campy themes and anthems from the WWF/WWE's 30-year reign of terror.

yum yum wontons

Every year, my friends the Perrys invite me to their house in Santa Fe to ring in the New Year. They buy lots of champagne, I blow up the kitchen—and a good time is had by all. On each visit I try to outdo the last with a mix of my latest recipes and greatest hits. One year I invited a romantic interest to join the melee. She graciously offered to make dessert wontons, as taught to her by her Japanese grandmother. To make a depressing story short, her wontons stole the show. Moral of the story: If you can't beat 'em, beg for their recipe. And so I did.

2 tablespoons butter

2 mangos, peeled, pitted, and finely diced

2 tablespoons coarsely peeled and grated fresh ginger

2¼ cups cognac

⅓ cup crystallized ginger, finely chopped

Twelve 3½-inch square wonton wrappers

¼ cup cornstarch

3 cups peanut oil for frying

¼ cup powdered sugar for dusting

In a sauté pan over medium-high heat, melt butter. Add mangos and fresh ginger, and sauté for approximately 5 minutes, or until they begin to brown. Add cognac, let it heat for 5 seconds, then ignite with a flame. Stand back! If flame does not burn out after 10 seconds, smother with a lid. Remove from heat and let cool. Stir in crystallized ginger and reserve.

Place a small bowl of warm water beside wonton wrappers. Lightly dust a baking sheet with cornstarch. Put a single wonton wrapper in the palm of your hand and spoon 1 tablespoon of mango mixture into the center. DO NOT OVERSTUFF. Dip fingers in the water (think of it as glue) and run it around all 4 edges of the wrapper. Fold wrapper in half on the diagonal like a turnover and press the edges tightly to seal the deal. If any tears appear in the wrapper, dump out the contents and start over. Set the finished wontons on the baking sheet. Do not let them touch one another. If you are not going to fry the wontons immediately, cover with a damp dish towel and refrigerate.

continued

Pour peanut oil into a tall pot or heavy skillet until it is 1 inch deep. Heat oil to 350°F (see Fear of Frying, page 126). Fry as many wontons at one time as your skillet will accommodate—without letting them touch. Fry for 30 seconds, or until the bottoms are golden brown. Then turn over for 30 more seconds, or until top sides are the same color. Remove with a slotted spoon and transfer to paper towels to drain excess oil. Proceed to next batch.

Place powdered sugar in a small strainer and hold strainer over wontons. Tap strainer gently to lightly dust wontons. Let cool for a couple of minutes before serving in a Chinese take-out container.

uncommon goods wonton wrappers (available in Asian groceries and the refrigerated section of many grocery stores); Chinese take-out container

level of difficulty Just like making homemade ravioli—your first few attempts will end up in the slagheap, and after that it's smooth sailing.

active prep 40 minutes

cooking time 10 minutes

shortcuts Start with store-bought frozen mango.

advance work Wontons can be prepared up to a day in advance, or weeks in advance and frozen. If you are storing them in the fridge or freezer, dust with a thin layer of cornstarch to keep them from sticking to each other. If frozen, thaw first, then fry just before serving.

music to cook by Various Artists, *Yummy Yummy: Best of Bubblegum Music* is a guilty pleasure from K-Tel.

liquid assets Once the cognac bottle is at hand, spill a little into some glasses and treat your guests to one of life's sublime pleasures.

fodder

fear of frying (a deep-frying tutorial)

Sure, deep-fried food may be bad for us, but that's why it's so good. And when used judiciously, it can accent your menu and broaden your culinary repertoire.

You don't need a deep fryer to make fried food at home. I don't have one. All it takes is a deep pot or pan, some oil, and a healthy respect for a combustible liquid that is almost twice the temperature of boiling water.

In the world of deep frying, oil temperature rules. The ideal frying temperature for the foods in this book is 350°–360°F. If the temperature is too high, food burns; too low and it will be greasy. The easiest way to maintain an ideal frying temperature (other than having a deep fryer) is to monitor the oil with an oil or candy thermometer—a worthy $20 investment. If you don't have one, stick a $1/2$-inch cube of bread on a fork or skewer and dip it in the oil. If the oil bubbles but the bread doesn't brown, the oil is not hot enough. If the bread browns instantly, the oil temperature is too high. And if the bread turns into a golden crouton in 5 to 10 seconds, you are set to fry.

Depending on the amount of oil you are using and the amount and density of the food you are frying, the oil temperature will likely spike momentarily, then drop as the frying process begins. Adjust your heat source accordingly to get back to 350°F as quickly as possible.

Everyone's pots and pans are different, but most will work. The ideal frying pot is a tall 2-quart pot. The ideal oil depth is 2–3 inches. Notwithstanding any instructions in this book, never fill the pot or pan more than one-third full. Oil has a tendency to bubble up vigorously as food is added. Keeping in mind what I said about not needing a deep fryer, if you get hooked on deep-fried pickles, Twinkies, or whatnot, you might consider investing in one of the many inexpensive consumer models available at cooking and department stores everywhere. Frying fans with commitment issues should pick up a fry basket or Chinese spider (about $3 apiece).

Peanut oil, with its high smoking point, is perfectly suited for deep frying, but any other vegetable oil can be used. You can reuse cooked oil several times. After each use, let the oil cool, then save it in the original (empty) bottle. A $1 funnel will be your new favorite kitchen tool, and if you want to be really fancy, stick a bit of cheesecloth in the bottom of it to strain out the sediment. Store oil in a cool dark place. You'll know your oil is spent when it starts smoking at normal temperatures or the color darkens substantially.

Hot oil is *verrrry* dangerous. Never leave it unattended on the stove. The best way to put out an oil fire (God forbid) is to smother it with a tightly fitting lid. Or, run a cloth under the tap, wring it out, and cover the flaming pan. Never throw water over burning oil and never attempt to move a burning pan. There, now go fry away.

proper handling of advance-prepped ingredients

* When following my hints for advance work, use common sense and refrigerate all perishable ingredients such as meat or dairy. Wrap them in plastic wrap or store in airtight containers. Ingredients that do not require refrigeration should also be stored in plastic wrap or airtight containers.
* Always marinate in the refrigerator, unless specifically directed otherwise.
* Refrigerated precooked ingredients that are not being reheated should be allowed to rise to room temperature before being served.

raw and coddled eggs

People with health problems, the very young, seniors, pregnant women, other high-risk groups, and leaders of the free world should not consume foods made with eggs that are not fully cooked, because there is a very, very slim chance of contracting salmonella poisoning.

Coddling diminishes the risks involved in using raw egg yolks by killing the bacteria without cooking the yolk. (For the record, the U.S.D.A. says no one should eat raw or coddled eggs, but I often do.) Start with blemish-free eggs that have been properly refrigerated. Submerge the whole egg in a pot of boiling water for exactly 40 seconds. Then remove, chill in cold water, and separate the yolk from the white as usual.

wine for the road

It is no secret that I am a devoted fan of the grape, and I believe that wine and spirits are an integral part of the dining experience (although I respectfully acknowledge, not for everybody). How much you choose to drink is your own deal, but driving after overindulging is everybody's problem. If your conscience doesn't convince you to leave your car at home, or at the party, consider the fact that the total cost of all the taxi rides will never add up to the retainer you will have to fork over to an attorney once you get caught.

suggested menus

this is a stick-up
coconut shrimp lollypops

maple salmon suckers

chicken popsicles

chorizo corn pups

lemongrass licks

asian fusion
haiku halibut

samurai scallops

chinese snow cones

lucky duck

yum yum wontons

summer sampler
cucumber shooters

margarita ceviche

byzantine bruschetta

chorizo corn pups

honey do shooters

romantic
psychedelic caviar

nest eggs

lovin' spoonfuls

bee stings

pearls of wisdom

high concept
gazpacholé

nest eggs

chinese snow cones

inside-out BLTs

fish cakes

egg creams

easy
psychedelic caviar

cocktail dates

goose mousse

cauliflower popcorn

bee stings

ice breakers

fancypants
psychedelic caviar

samurai scallops

maple salmon suckers

foie gras & jam

pearls of wisdom

bbq
finger-lickin' shrimp

maple salmon suckers

gaucho snacks

bang-bang drummettes

s'more shooters

praise

Elizabeth Karmel for helping me see that there was a book in my obsession with bites.
Aynsley Vogel for adding her touch of class to the written word.
Suzi Varin for her creative eye and contagious enthusiasm.
Suzanne Janke for being part of the adventure.
Norman Perry and Monica Netupsky for standing by your boy.
Jane Dystel for getting it.
Bill LeBlond for saying yes.
Rodney Bowes for being Rodney.

kitchen cabinet David Sanfield, Marta Pan, Elizabeth Karmel, Karrie Galvin, Mary Sue Milliken, Fred Eric, Mary Burnham, Romily Perry, Rodney Bowes, Randy St. Clair, Nate Allen, and all of the unofficial tasters of Rutherford Drive   **wine cabinet** Suzanne Janke, Kelly Bernard, Elena Morelli   **record cabinet** Susan Rose, Trent Tomlinson

Dale Burshtein, Beth Fanjoy, Richard Mortimer, and the whole crew from my show
Mary Beth McAdaragh and Ted Eccles
Everyone at Food Network Canada and Food Network (U.S.A)
Alison Emilio, "Gaucho" Jack Blumer, Sarah Damson, Matt Zimbel, Andrew Zimbel, "Aisha," Jow, Charisse Glenn, Lesley Hollenberg, Angela Freire, John & Dede, Noah Edelstein, Mimi, Sang Kim, Al Dechellis, Ronda Locke

The kitchen staff at Campanile, L.A., and Craft, N.Y.C., who let me slice, dice, and glean.
My kindred culinary spirits who allow me to remain on this path by supporting my surreal endeavors.
And to all the farmers, winemakers, and culinary artisans who sweeten life's rich pagent.

sources Love Plates (all the gorgeous translucent and polka-dot glass plates and bowls), French Bull (the fantabulous contemporary melamine plates), Illy (espresso cups), Sherri Hay (fauxtoshopped labels), Chris Crouse (Plexiglas trays), Smart & Final (paper cups), Melissa Castro (custom printing).

All photographed food prepared, styled, and eaten by Bob Blumer.
For books, limited edition prints, and other information on adventures in entertaining with the surreal gourmet:

call 1 800-FAUX-PAS   surf www.surrealgourmet.com   e-mail gastronaut@surrealgourmet.com
mail The Surreal Gourmet, P.O. Box 2961, Hollywood, CA, USA 90078

index